PEARSON

At Pearson, we believe in learning – all kinds of learning for all kinds of people. Whether it's at home, in the classroom or in the workplace, learning is the key to improving our life chances.

That's why we're working with leading authors to bring you the latest thinking and the best practices, so you can get better at the things that are important to you. You can learn on the page or on the move, and with content that's always crafted to help you understand quickly and apply what you've learned.

If you want to upgrade your personal skills or accelerate your career, become a more effective leader or more powerful communicator, discover new opportunities or simply find more inspiration, we can help you make progress in your work and life.

Pearson is the world's leading learning company. Our portfolio includes the Financial Times, Penguin, Dorling Kindersley, and our educational business, Pearson International.

Every day our work helps learning flourish, and wherever learning flourishes, so do people.

To learn more please visit us at: www.pearson.com/uk

Ouch!

Ignorance is bliss,
except when it hurts

PAUL KNOTT

PEARSON

Harlow, England • London • New York • Boston • San Francisco • Toronto • Sydney
Auckland • Singapore • Hong Kong • Tokyo • Seoul • Taipei • New Delhi
Cape Town • São Paulo • Mexico City • Madrid • Amsterdam • Munich • Paris • Milan

PEARSON EDUCATION LIMITED

Edinburgh Gate
Harlow CM20 2JE
Tel: +44 (0)1279 623623
Fax: +44 (0)1279 431059
Website: www.pearson.com/uk

First published in Great Britain in 2012

Pearson Education is not responsible for the content of third-party internet sites.

ISBN: 978-0-273-77292-7

British Library Cataloguing-in-Publication Data
A catalogue record for this book is available from the British Library

Library of Congress Cataloging-in-Publication Data
A catalog record for this book is available from the Library of Congress.

10 9 8 7 6 5 4 3 2 1
16 15 14 13 12

Designed by Design Deluxe

Typeset in 10/13pt Sabon Ltd Std by 3
Printed and bound in Great Britain by Ashford Colour Press Ltd, Gosport, Hampshire

To Ken and Elva

For the love, the nurture and for just letting me get on with being the rogue gene

Contents

About the author

Paul Knott does not work in the finance industry, he's one of us. Someone who has a passion for helping others make the most of what they have. A business turnaround specialist, he is no stranger to protecting people's money in a crisis. Paul has a degree in Mathematics from the University of London and a Masters in Retail Marketing from TIAS Business School in the Netherlands. He currently resides beachside in Whitstable, and Brazil.

Publisher's acknowledgements

We are grateful to the following for permission to reproduce copyright material:

Cartoons

Cartoon on p.31 from Married to the Sea http://www.married tothesea.com/, Drew and Natalie Dee.

Figures

Figures on pp.90, 98, 104, 105 (bottom), 127, 178 from *MoneyWeek*, http://www.moneyweek.com; Figure on p.102 from Bank of England, http://www.bankofengland.co.uk; Figure on p.105 (top) from www.nationwide.co.uk; Figure on p.129 from Westcore Funds, www.westcore.com, Westcore Funds; Figure on p.131 from Dr Jean-Paul Rodrigue, Hofstra University; Figure on p.153 from Professor Robert Shiller, Yale University; Figures on pp.188, 190, 192, 196 from Gold and Silver.com, http://goldsilver.com, Gold & Silver, Inc.; Figure on p.223 from Examiner.com, 'The tyranny-liberty cycle of government', Ann Miller, 8 June 2009; Figure on p.215 from Chris Martenson. com, www.chrismartenson.com, Chris Martenson.

Text

Letter on p.143 from 'Readers' letters', *Guardian*, 8 November 2008 (Castles, C.).

Picture Credits

Alamy Images: Ilene MacDonald / Alamy p.9, Steve Allen Travel Photography / Alamy / Reserve Bank of Zimbabwe p.12, Thomas Lehne / lotuseaters / Alamy p.26; Bert Folsom / Alamy p.35; **Andy Dao and Ivan Cash:** p.33; **Molly Crabapple INC:** p.44; **Science Photo Library Ltd:** National Library of Medicine / Science Photo Library p.119; **This Ain't Rock 'n' Roll Ltd:** p.212.

All other images © Pearson Education

In some instances we have been unable to trace the owners of copyright material, and we would appreciate any information that would enable us to do so.

Author's acknowledgements

THE FIRST WORD OF THANKS goes to someone who to my great regret, is no longer around to see the book come to fruition. Marshall was there way before any thoughts of committing finger to keyboard had emerged and many a lively monetary discussion was undertaken in Covent Garden aided and abetted by whichever of the three stimulants were closest to hand. Always laughter, often caffeine but his true weapon of choice was wet, Czech and always above a 5 per cent interest rate. We lost one of the good guys. Sorely missed, but never forgotten.

Books sometimes need hard times, serendipity or a catalyst, mine required all three. Look at the damage you have done Mr Lister with that one telephone call? So I will always be indebted to you for making the connection and for providing such a serene writing environment of asbestos, brick dust and mostly no floor. However this was more than compensated, by ensuring I did not die of frostbite, via limitless free coffees and culinary delights served up by your unique team at Samphire Restaurant.

And I shouldn't forget to mention my personal soup kitchen, a.k.a. The Deli, thanks David.

Next up are two special ladies who were stupid enough to think this was ever going to be a runner. Isy *'Miss Power Lipstick'* Atherton at Creative Authors and Commissioning Editor Rachael *'no that's far too rude we will have to cut it'* Stock. Clearly you are both stark raving bonkers and I love you for displaying a backbone and taking this twisted bull by the horns. And that also goes East to you Paul, to Laura, Elie and all the team at Pearson who I presume are now actively seeking alternative employment opportunities.

When you are toying with nonsense it is often wise to have a proper grown-up in charge. Anthony, thanks for your support and almost keeping me on the straight and narrow as far as the dismal science is concerned. I have no doubt marred your career by association but I appreciate the sacrifice and of course for keeping 'the Faithy'. And not forgetting Ben for being on the money at the last minute.

Other thanks go to Iain Laurie – the original 'Mr Paralytically Incorrect', Jon Hanks, and Anthony at Palamedes for t'interweb stuff, Andy at Mosley Design for the brilliant cover and yet another graphic liberty on my part. To Ben Dixon for the graphic liberty on your part. To Rob and Amie for last minute emergency writing accommodation and to Sarah, Cakes, Wigs, Sheila, Erin, Detlef, Jeremy, Mel, Andre, Rene, Nid and anyone else who supported bringing this to book. To all my long standing friends. The last words go to an old 'mentor(-list)'; Slap – you should have trained me better – GFY.

Disclaimer: Please note that I am not a financial adviser. Any actions or decisions you take regarding your money and investments are entirely your responsibility.

Attribution note: Obviously when you are taking a tour around the monetary universe there are a lot of sages and words of wisdom to embrace. I trust I have given all due attribution where appropriate and if I have missed anyone then my humblest apologies.

Introduction

YOU MAY BE FANTASTIC as a friend/at work/in bed/ on fire (delete as inappropriate) but how are you when it comes to finance? There seems to be this huge disconnect for a large number of otherwise capable and intelligent human beings with respect to money. We are all interested at one level (spending it!) but when it comes to learning more about how to master it, well ... let's just say, *everybody's shufflin'*. We know we *ought* to but does anyone actually *want* to? Want is good, ought is nought. Well, this blasé approach has had relatively few consequences to date but the rules of the game have changed – maybe without you even noticing? You are now facing a *potential* wipe-out and regardless of whether or not the worst comes to pass, isn't your money too important to be left 'unattended' with incompetent bankers and the parasitical finance industry? If you think the answer to that last question is yes, then you may wish to continue.

Let's tell it like it is. With finance there is a real fear of the unknown (or is that the bewildering?), and perhaps fear of embarrassment – that you'll expose your slight lack of knowledge and come out looking like a 'Tim, nice but dim' character. Procrastination rules, and the available literature mostly turns us into world champion narcoleptics before the end of the first page – it's about as exciting as watching a river erode. The truth is, it is not just for one of the above reasons that we don't do more, it's for *'all of the above'* reasons. If any of this resonates with your own behaviour then you are going to need a little help.

If these were the only barriers we faced it would be bad enough, but on top of all that we like to abdicate responsibility in the face of 'expertise' and blindly follow advice without questioning the source. Imagine you are a circus knife-thrower who gets it wrong 97 per cent of the time. Chances are that your career might be almost as short-lived as your assistants. But this level of inaccuracy is regularly on display within the mainstream media. Errors of judgement abound but, unlike the circus act, the people throwing – in this case their opinions – are rarely, if ever, held accountable. Not only does this allow them to carry on getting it consistently wrong but far worse, if you act on the advice, it is likely to make you poor, very quickly.

But is predicting the future absolutely impossible for anybody? This is a question that will be revisited in more depth later but to deny it completely is to disregard *cause* and *effect*, or *action* and *re-action*, which would be a mistake. For example, if I were to go and kick any dog in the street tomorrow it is almost guaranteed that I will be barked at and it is possible that I would be bitten on the leg. It's not guaranteed but one can say with some certainty it is likely to happen. What can be said is that the probability of being bitten by the dog has increased dramatically by taking the preceding action. It is this level of consequential thinking combined with some fascinating repetitive patterns and human failings (not involving abuse of man's best friend) that will allow us to see that the future isn't always as opaque as it first appears.

We will be ruthlessly applying Occam's razor. This is not some medieval contraption from the Spanish inquisition – tempting as it may sound to any sadists – but a principle attributed to the 14th century English logician and Franciscan friar, William of Occam which is often summarised as: 'All other things being equal, the simplest explanation is the best.'

So that's the aim of this book; to demystify the whole approach to finance, to give you an urgent wake-up call to what's really happening with your money and to put a smile on your face without putting you to sleep. As an informed layperson you can prosper as long as you follow some simple rules. This will allow you to blissfully ignore the vast majority of so-called financial experts. In fact, the more you ignore most of this group the more successful you will become. And while there are plenty of analogies, irreverence, and simplicity for the fiscally challenged there is enough insight and gravitas that it should also appeal to the more accomplished.

Before we significantly improve your financial acumen (and possibly stop you from being ruined) there are three foundations stones that need to be put in place. Our journey starts by following the money and pulling its pants down. That's right, a full exposure of what it really is, who controls it and why lots of people who should be suitably embarrassed aren't. Then we move on to the human psyche. Why? Because to understand the investment arena you first have to know the weaknesses and flaws that are hardwired into the human brain. The third foundation stone is quality of information. An analysis of the press demonstrates why so many of us are poor at investing – we are listening to the wrong sources. The good news is this is easily amended. The book then proceeds to give a practical hands-on and brains-on guide on what to do about it, and we also take time out to debunk a few myths along the way.

One of the few silver linings to emerge is the opportunity to use 'le crunch' as a case study to explain how money really works and its interconnection with our own behaviour. The reality is that the financial slow motion train wreck is far from over and the repercussions will reverberate for years to come. People are more willing to listen, learn and take action after an event has occurred than before it. That alas is one of our human foibles.

So who am I to tell you what you need to know? And am I cheating by writing with the benefit of hindsight (how easy is that)? The insight given is not just a rationalisation after the event. By taking personal proactive action in 2007, following the principles outlined in this book, I ensured no loss on my investments during 2008 despite the market dropping 38 per cent. That's definitely above average performance. So if you want to know how to preserve and grow your money, even in a crisis, this book will show you.

As for 'Why listen to me?', well, maybe I'm like you (as long as you are not a raging psycho with a penchant for tiddlywinks). I'm not a financial professional. I'm not a financial advisor, nor have I ever worked for a bank. Neither am I an analyst or fund manager. And aside from a small proportion of the cover price I have absolutely nothing to gain personally from what I share with you here. I'm not defending myself or, like some, propping up the system that feeds me. And whilst I have enough high grade qualifications to fill a pram, I don't have an academic reputation to protect and no one to impress apart from Rocco, the Jack Russell, and he is usually sated with a biscuit. That means we are free to go for a rollicking tour as opposed to just a trudge around the monetary universe.

So why do I want to share what I've learned with you? First, because I like to side with the underdog and, trust me, when it comes to the finance industry you are not just the underdog – you are the host. Secondly, while I have countless failings to my name, I'm a sucker for sharing information and enjoy taking the supposedly complex and making it simple for others. I have set up my own businesses and helped others successfully turn around theirs, so I know how hard it can be to generate cash in the first place and thus feel anyone who has managed to do that (or as we will see, even those who haven't) shouldn't have it stolen from them just because they do not know how the system really works. As it says on the cover, *'Ignorance is bliss – except when it hurts'*. I want you to see the 'Ouch!' so you don't have to feel it.

If you really would like to know what is going on with your money you simply need to turn the page …

'*Down one road lies disaster, down the other utter catastrophe.*
Let us hope we have the wisdom to choose wisely.'

Woody Allen

CHAPTER 1

Show me the money

Its origins and how it works

The study of money, above all other fields in economics, is one in which complexity is used to disguise truth or to evade truth, not to reveal it JOHN KENNETH GALBRAITH

A sound banker, alas, is not one who foresees danger and avoids it, but one who, when he is ruined, is ruined in a conventional way along with his fellows, so that no one can really blame him JOHN MAYNARD KEYNES

MONEY, THAT'S WHAT I WANT

Money: all of us use it, most people would like more of it; some believe it makes us happier, others think it is the root of all evil and, allegedly, it makes the world go around. Have we become too fixated by it or should we be more interested in it? Regardless of how much or how little you have, are you actively making the most of yours?

When many of us think of money, we immediately visualise pieces of paper that happen to have a picture of a famous dead person or historical event on one side and on the other an image of the President or Totalitarian Dictator (one and the same in some cases) depending on which part of the planet you reside. Physical currency in the UK represents only 3 per cent of the total funds in circulation. In order to deal with the complexities of modern money, and credit, it is worth reminding ourselves of its origins and its fundamental use.

PREHISTORIC TRANSACTIONS

Ted and Ugg are cavemen. Ted hunts woolly mammoths as shaggy dogs have yet to evolve. Ugg runs the local hardware hut making spears. There is a good supply of woolly mammoths. Ted will 'sell' two woolly mammoths in order to 'buy' one new spear from Ugg.

Ugg's lover Terra decides she would like a new painting on the wall of their cave. Ugg is frankly rubbish at drawing but knows someone called Stig in the next village. Stig's crib is no dump. He's an aspiring Michelangelo (or at least he would be if he had been born 30,000 years later). Stig, unusually for a caveman, hates violence and cannot bear spears (a rare syndrome that reappeared in the 21st century). Ugg therefore has a problem; he can't 'buy' Stig's cave painting services as he has nothing to 'sell' to Stig. However Stig does need to eat. His village's woolly mammoth hunter was trampled to death last week so he's pretty hungry. Ugg being an ingenious sort of chap decides he will pay for the picture by doing a side deal with Ted, the woolly mammoth hunter. Ugg and Stig agree that one mammoth is worth one cave painting. So Ugg could make an agreement that instead of providing spears to Stig, he would barter with Ted to send over a woolly mammoth instead. Ugg will compensate Ted, with half a spear (remember two woolly mammoths = one spear). Ted is not very happy, as half a spear is fairly useless – especially when you get the blunt end of the stick.

It is concluded that they need a smaller denomination that they can all agree on. Stig suggests they could use sexual favours instead, say one night of passion with Ugg's lover Terra = quarter of a woolly mammoth. All agree this is a great unit of exchange (sexism was apparently rife) but this fails to take off when Terra points out she considers her services are worth at least a whole herd of woolly mammoths. After a lot of hair pulling and clubbing each other they decide they need a system that:

1   Allows them to avoid this complex and unruly exchange process.

2   Offers a standard unit of exchange.

3   Is accepted by everyone and that they have faith in it.

Money evolved from the need to satisfy these points. Money essentially attempts to cover five functions: it should be a *medium*, a *measure*, and a *standard*, it needs to be *portable*, and it offers a *store* of *value*. It usually manages the first four quite well but often fails on the last point. Let's return to our friendly cave-dwellers to see why:

Ted is unhappy; he's been so successful in his woolly mammoth killing exploits that finding them has now become very difficult. As a result Ugg and Stig are starving and desperate. Spears and paintings are losing value with nothing to eat. Ugg and Stig decide to offer ten cave paintings and five spears to Ted if he can capture one woolly mammoth before nightfall. Ted, inspired by this incentive and the possibility of attracting an alpha female cave-dweller by owning the most beautiful cave in town hunts down said woolly mammoth and is therefore able to take delivery of the spears and painting services. Clearly there has been a rapid change in the value of things because of a change of circumstances. Ted is happy; the others are relieved but somewhat poorer.

The following week a massive new herd of mammoths arrives. Ted now has so much woolly mammoth meat he doesn't know what to do with it. His alpha female mate is very demanding and she wants the whole cave finished off with beautiful paintings. He asks Stig to do this but Stig has eaten so much woolly mammoth he can't be bothered getting out of bed. So Ted has to offer ten woolly mammoths just to get one cave painting.

This simplistic example demonstrates one very important point which still applies in today's society; whatever is being used as money, or is being used to back money, its **value** has often proven to be changeable over time. This aspect of money is unsatisfactory and of course open to abuse. Unfortunately no one has invented any simpler or more flexible alternatives.

Many items have been used as money including, bricks, barley, feathers, jewellery, livestock etc. It just had to fulfil the five criteria set out above. Gold became popular because it was visually attractive, malleable, divisible, inert and limited in supply. This last aspect gave people faith in the metal and this meant it was relatively stable. However, gold and other precious metals also have their limitations when used as money, but let's use gold to explain how the banking system was invented. The reality of the situation may come as a rude awakening to those not familiar with it. In fact some readers may think it positively outrageous.

ORIGIN OF FAECES

Let's go back in time to before banks existed and imagine you are a traditional goldsmith* in ye olde workshop crafting a living. You buy raw gold and silver and forge it into various items such as goblets and bling-bling jewellery. More importantly, you are responsible for casting coins of certified weight and purity to be used as money for the exchange of goods and services.

In order to protect your gold supplies from pilferers, general riff raff and ne'er-do-wells all looking for a ten-fingered discount, you decide to build a vault in which to store it. This cunning security manoeuvre doesn't go unnoticed and others who own gold and silver decide they would also like to deposit their money in a secure location. It seems they have a wide choice of two locations – the haystack or your vault. So naturally your astute business brain kicks into gear and recognises the window of opportunity to charge a fee for warehousing their gold as well as yours. Business is looking up.

Your ability to store the gold gives your depositors an additional benefit because whilst the coins are relatively portable, carrying lots of heavy gold or silver coins is still cumbersome and an inconvenience. Now, to keep track of who owns what you write a ledger and give depositors a paper ticket or claim note as proof of ownership. This allows them to reclaim their gold on demand. Over time, because the paper receipts issued are far more portable than the gold and because everyone knows they are backed by physical gold in the vault they become accepted as money. This 'commodity money' system seems to work and there is trust in it.

In addition to minting coins and renting out space in your vault, you develop another side to the business – namely, making loans to people. These loans are used in order to trade goods and services. By lending out your gold reserves you are able to charge a small rate of interest on it. Business is looking even better.

*Goldsmith story adapted from the work of Paul Grignon, Murray Rothbard et al.

Some of your borrowers take the loan in gold but many are happy to accept the loan from you in the form of paper claim notes instead of the actual metal as everyone has faith in them. Over time this becomes the de facto method of trading, with the gold rarely leaving the vault.

At this point you decide to get creative and with only a smidgen of duplicity you spot an opportunity to increase your wealth. As few borrowers now take loans in actual gold, why not write claim notes against the depositors' gold as well as your own? No one will notice as long as the loans are repaid. This will allow you to make greater profits than by lending just your own gold. **What could possibly go wrong?**

This system works well for some time until one night, down at ye olde inn, you are persuaded to imbibe one flagon of mead too many and you let slip your extended business concept. Eventually more people find out what has been happening and aren't best pleased.

Initially depositors are annoyed at you gaining interest on their gold but subsequently many realise this is actually a business opportunity. Instead of lynching you, depositors decide they want a piece of the action. An agreement is reached so that depositors receive part of the interest you are charging on their own gold. You set a rate with respect to the depositor's gold which you then loan out at a higher rate. You are no longer just a goldsmith, you are now a fully fledged banker. The essence of banking is essentially just this, borrowing at a low rate of interest and lending at a higher one.

THE ULTIMATE CONFIDENCE TRICK

As trade is booming, and more people want loans, there is pressure to further increase credit levels. Now this is where your banker's creative juices go into overdrive and up pops the mother of all brainwaves. It just requires an equal and opposite decrease in your moral fibre as you put your principles to one side and drop kick them through the arched window.*

You already noticed from past experience depositors rarely came to the vault to demand the physical gold and never all at the same time. As no one knows how much gold is actually in the vault you decide to issue extra claim notes on gold that doesn't exist and charge interest on it – simple!

Instead of all the paper claim notes being 100 per cent backed by real gold, in the vaults now only a *fraction* of the total written ledger is backed by gold *reserves*. Welcome to fractional reserve banking. Banking had become a confidence trick. The power to invent money out of thin air had been established. It's time for those immortal words, '**what could possibly go wrong?**'

Eventually, of course, word got out (it is apparently hard to keep a good story down). Not surprisingly, borrowers demanded physical gold instead of paper IOUs. Queues formed outside the bank. The bank naturally did not have enough gold to redeem all the receipts that had been put into circulation, the bank was insolvent. This is called 'a run on the bank' and has led to the demise of numerous independent banks throughout history. Many of us now have personal experience of this phenomenon as it happened in 2007 for the first time in the UK for 130 years, courtesy of Northern Rock. These original bank runs ruined public confidence in bankers (sounding familiar, anyone?).

Limits were agreed on the amount of fictional loan money that could be created. It would be larger than the actual amount of gold in the vaults but it would be set at a fixed ratio to it e.g. banks must keep 10 per cent of the amount they had lent out in reserve. Fractional reserve banking (or variations of it) became the dominant money system in the world. We will revisit this point shortly but immediately it's clear there is at least one problem with it. The whole system is inherently unstable. If

* George Selgin has recently argued that the original goldsmiths may have just had a bad press.

8
OUCH!

everyone asks for their money back at the same time, the system collapses!

EMPTY PROMISES

As trade has expanded so has the size of the confidence trick. Instead of just inventing fake money backed by a tangible asset we have 'progressed'! The fractional reserve percentage has not only been reduced over time but the backing has also fallen off. It was decided that instead of backing the currency notes issued with something tangible such as gold or silver, the system would be changed to a Fiat system, which is essentially backed by just a promise. Fiat (meaning 'let it be done' in Latin) is merely a decree laid down by the government of the day that there is a promise to repay the holder of the note, in more paper money. Legal tender laws state that citizens must accept this as payment for debt. Compare the two notes below:

1957 US bank note: promise to pay in silver

New US bank note: promise to pay in paper

So what, you might say? Does anyone or should anyone care about it? After all, the Fiat system appears to have facilitated a global boom, especially in the 20th century. Well, the answer to this question is yes. Why? Because every paper or Fiat money system ever invented in the history of mankind has failed over time. Why? Lack of self-control; without limitation or anything tangible backing it, the temptation to 'print' as much as you would like is too great. Voltaire, in the 18th century, summed up the problem:

> 66 *Paper money eventually returns to its intrinsic value – zero.* 99

Money 'printing', of course, has relevance today because this approach has been adopted by many countries and may have far-reaching implications for your personal wealth. The official banking term for printing money is 'quantitative easing'. Why? It's that modern disease called 'nomenclature easing' rearing its ugly head again; the incessant tendency to rename things in order for them to be either:

1   Less offensive.

2   More confusing to the uninitiated.

Perhaps 'printing money' sounds just a bit too obvious or villainous?

Of course from a technical perspective experts will say 'quantitative easing' has nothing to do with 'printing physical money'. Money can be put into circulation electronically by central banks but the end effect is almost identical, so the argument stands. Of course politicians use the difference to spin and distract without lying. It's the same argument as Bill Clinton's infamous line, *'I did not have sex with that woman'*. It is only true on a sublime technicality.

It's worth remembering when all is said and done, money, be it cave paintings, gold, paper or anything else, is only a medium to facilitate the exchange of goods of real value. This paper note in the end has to represent something tangible because the 'paper' itself is worthless. In the paper money printing world you might think:

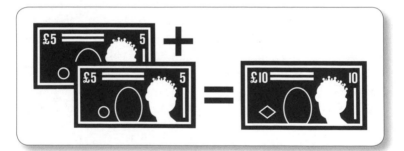

It doesn't. **Double** the *total* money supply overnight and you will **halve** the value of it, so in fact:

How disappointing! But why?

Imagine that you are a counterfeiter producing £5 notes. You are so good at your chosen profession that no-one can tell the difference between the fake £5 and the real £5. You print lots of £5 notes and start spending them. This has two effects:

1   The total money supply of the country increases, thus driving up prices, because the purchasing power of the existing currency unit is decreased. This decrease is directly proportional to the amount of fake cash you put into circulation.

2   You get richer whilst everyone else gets poorer. It changes the wealth distribution because whilst there is a general lowering of purchasing power per currency unit there is a disproportionate amount of money in your hands as the counterfeiter. **If you are first in the chain you get the benefit.**

The same reasoning is valid if the 'counterfeiter' happens to be the government. By diluting the total by printing money it also acts as a wealth transfer mechanism to the state at the expense of the general populous. Even if you do not have any savings it lowers the value of your existing wages because they no longer buy what they once did. It's just you don't notice it because it happens over a period of time. Covert daylight robbery, anyone?

To highlight the point let's look at that bastion of fiscal control, Zimbabwe. Zimbabwe is not a world leader in many activities but it had by 2008 become expert in inflation and money printing. Inflation there was running at an astonishing 13.2 billion per cent a month, meaning Zimbabwe's annual rate of inflation in November 2008 was 516 quintillion per cent. That's 516 followed by 18 noughts (516, 000, 000, 000, 000, 000, 000). Prices were doubling every 1.3 days! Inflation levels in this African nation were on course to exceed Hungary's 1946 world record, where prices doubled every 15.6 hours.

You know you are in trouble when you own a wheelbarrow full of money and the wheelbarrow is more valuable than the contents. Zimbabwean dollars, it is fair to say are no longer a great *store* of value. This happens when governments think they can escape debt by printing money. It's not only despots that get desperate.

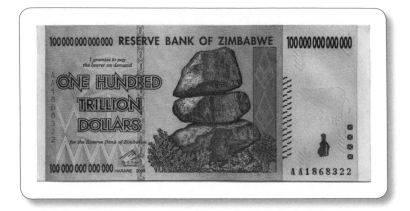

Couldn't happen in the UK? Well you can argue the camouflage for that path is already installed. The government's Banking Bill of 2009 abolished a law that has been in place since 1844 which obliges the Bank of England to publish a weekly account of its balance sheet. Financial rules are put in place for a reason and they are taken away for another reason, usually the wrong one.

The escapology solution of choice for Zimbabwe was obvious – adopt the world's reserve currency, the US dollar as its principal trading notes. Problem solved then? Jump forward three years to 2011, after the US Federal Reserve has massively expanded the money supply, and the Harare *Financial Gazette* asks, '*Should Zimbabwe be worried [about the US dollar]*'. Cue the usual John McEnroe quote. It's a bit of a rum do when the inhabitants of the worst run monetary system in the world start to worry about the world's 'safe haven' currency.

So before you swear your undying allegiance to Fiat money you may want to bear in mind Kenneth J. Gerbino's take on it: 'Do you trust the logic of taking a pine tree, worth

$4,000–$5,000, cutting it up, turning it into pulp, putting some ink on it and then calling it one billion dollars?' (Urban myth alert: they actually make dollars out of cotton and linen, Ken, but let's not split hairs on the minor detail.)

Money 'printing' (it's mostly electronic nowadays) is so often the main *cause* of inflation. Think of it as the paper currency decreasing in value, not real items going up in price (it just seems that way because we tend to think that the medium of exchange is fixed because it has a fixed number on it, e.g. £5).

66 *Inflation is always and everywhere a monetary phenomenon.* 99 **Milton Freidman**

This raises the questions of where true value lies, what will be of real value in the future, and can you protect the money you already have? But before we dive into that particular barrel of fish let's finish what we've started and try to understand this fictional money system a little more.

HOW FICTIONAL MONEY IS CREATED

Before moving on to harnessing the real power of money for ourselves, we should at least make an attempt at explaining how much of the 'fictional' money is brought into existence today. We'll start with how it used to work and then add in a little twist of modern romance to bring it up to date. Let's keep things as simple as possible and avoid too many technicalities.

There are essentially two types of money:

● Central bank money (physical currency and other reserves).

● Commercial bank money (customer deposits and 'money' created through loans) – sometimes called **chequebook** money.

Let's target the second one first, e.g. high street banks. Stay focused, because we are about to magic money from nowhere.

Some people believe that when you put your money in a bank it stays in your deposit account for when you want to withdraw it. Wrong. You are in fact 'loaning' your money to the bank with a promise from the bank to pay it back on demand. In law, it's still your asset but no longer your property.

Clearly banks do not just lend out other people's deposits because there are not enough deposits to go round. So how does a bank lend out money it doesn't have? Easy – it creates it electronically out of thin air. Who said abracadabra doesn't work? Take this example:

NB: for the purposes of this illustration the source of your deposit is newly minted extra money as a gift from the central bank – Happy Birthday!

Say you deposit £1,000 in a bank. Under the old rules of fractional reserve banking (assume a 10 per cent reserve ratio is required) the bank must keep £100 of that money in reserve. It is then free to lend out the other £900 to person B. Your original £1,000 is now split into £100 cash reserve and a £900 IOU from the bank with, it could be said for argument's sake, person B holding 'your' £900. In reality it doesn't matter which way you argue it but the total money supply has just increased. It is now £1,000 + £900 = £1,900. The bank loan to person B has generated £900 in brand new money in the form of debt. Of course under these precise circumstances if you want all your money back immediately the bank can't give it to you. The system only works in aggregate so that at any one time only a small percentage of people are demanding their deposits back, which is usually exactly what happens. So normally there is no problem, but remember, **you no longer own the money you have put in the bank**. This will come as a total surprise to exactly 74 per cent of the UK population.*

The good news for the banks is that not only can they do this loaning of your money once but they can do it multiple times. So say person B uses the loan to buy a sofa from person C and this £900 is then deposited by person C at a bank. The £900 loan has created another deposit. The bank puts 10 per cent in reserve (£90) and can then loan out the other £810. The money supply has now increased further. This process is allowed to happen over and over again in ever-decreasing circles meaning, in this case, the mathematics allows the original £1,000 to be grown into £10,000, but no more than this.

If you have made it to here, congratulations! You now know a lot more about our money system than the vast majority of people (including most MPs and bank employees). However, there are a couple of other nuances to absorb. First, the above example assumes the process starts with a customer deposit. This isn't strictly true. Banks can now lend without first receiving a deposit.

If you want to loan money to a friend you must first have that money in your account whereas a bank does not. This is the real abracadabra bit.

> **❝ *Banks extend credit by creating money.* ❞**
> **Paul Tucker, Deputy Governor of**
> **the Bank of England 2007**

If you go into a bank and obtain a loan this is brand new money (that did not exist before) created as debt with the borrower (you) promising to repay it in the future with the proceeds of your labour. The offer of the loan is based as much on the bank being convinced you can and will repay it as anything else. So your request for money triggers the money creation.

It is made up of the principal (the original loan amount) and interest (what you pay on top for the privilege of borrowing it).

---

* Public attitudes to banking survey by ESCP Europe for the Cobden Centre, June 2010.

Banks get to type into the system new money and charge interest on it.

> 66 *The process by which banks create money is so simple that the mind is repelled.* 99 **John Kenneth Galbraith**

So commercial banks get to create money ex nihilo (out of nothing) but there is 'in theory' a mathematical limit on how much. It used to be defined by the fractional reserve ratio but that was changed to be based on other factors. Don't worry we don't need to descend into that basket of vipers.

Hang on, you might be asking, where is the downside? Who wouldn't want a business where you can make interest on money you never had in the first place? George W. Ball certainly liked the sound of it when in the 1960s he left public office to be a partner in a Wall Street bank, proclaiming: *'Why, didn't someone tell me about banking before?'*

This 'money from nowhere' malarkey sounds like a right royal wheeze. The only restriction being that the commercial banks can create only so much debt. Or at least that's how it's supposed to work. In practice, in the UK, the modern 'restrictions' are bordering on the marginal. At the height of the crisis in 2008 UK banks had £1.25 in reserve for every £100 credit created. This sounds about as resilient as a chocolate teapot in the Gobi desert. **'What could possibly go wrong?'**

This system works 'perfectly well' when everything runs smoothly but as events have shown, that isn't always the case. Commercial banks have to be good risk assessors and not become greedy or complacent.

The government and/or the central bank, in our case the Bank of England, can on the other hand, literally create limitless money out of thin air as it is not subject to any fractional or capital reserve scheme whatsoever. This has been described by Murray Rothbard and others as 'legalised counterfeiting'. Well, who wouldn't be tempted to indulge in a bit of that given the opportunity? Before we delve any deeper into the counterfeiting we first need to make sure the force is with us ...

THE MOST POWERFUL FORCE IN THE UNIVERSE

66 *The most powerful force in the universe is compound interest.* 99 **A. Einstein** *

Compound boredom is the normal state of affairs when anyone mentions compound interest, or at least that's what many recall from their school-days. Perhaps it was the dryness of the delivery but when we have arguably the 20th century's cleverest guy making such a bold statement it is time to refresh our memories?

Imagine your name is Cecil (hard, but run with it) and you have a twin sister called Cecilia (your mum is good with money, and procreation, but not so hot with names). For your 16th birthday she offers you £10,000 every year until you retire at 65 and your sister just a one-off payment of £10,000. While you are running around the room doing high fives, Cecilia is in the corner crying her eyes out wondering why mum hates her so much.

The money comes with two small prerequisites. Neither of you can touch the money until your 65th birthday and whilst your money receives no interest, your sister's will receive some to compensate for the otherwise ultra harsh, draconian, one-sided deal.

Cecilia, being sharp with numbers, spots an opportunity and successfully negotiates with her mum a guaranteed annual interest rate of 10 per cent per year.

Time passes and you meet up for a family reunion after a decade and discuss your finances. As expected you are much

* If in doubt, attribute it to Einstein. He might have said it but its attribution remains murky.

better off. You have £100,000 banked and Cecilia only £23,000 from the original deal; she has over £75,000 less.

Now you have a grin on your face but you can't understand why your sister's grin appears to be imitating that of the Cheshire Cat. She knows she's going to get the last laugh and here is why ...

After 49 years it's time to collect your money, all £490,000 of it, but that scheming cow of a sister, Cecilia, has indeed broken your heart by netting £970,172 and suddenly you feel you should have paid a bit more attention during that compound boredom lesson. Compounding is an exponential function which in this case means the big money is made at the end. It's like the rabbit and the tortoise, except this tortoise has had a nitrous oxide tank strapped to its back after year 40.

With compound interest it's more about the amount of time (and the rate) than the amount of money. Even if it's small amounts, it's worth starting early. Make it work for you, not vice versa. It's kind of stupid not to (see the figure on the next page).

> 66 *The greatest shortcoming of the human race is our inability to understand the exponential function.* 99 **Albert A. Bartlett**

Now let's change the rate from 10 per cent to 30 per cent. If, say, a moneylender offers you £10,000 when you are 16 at an annual compound interest rate of 30 per cent, how much will you have to pay back when you retire 49 years later? Obviously it's higher than £970,172 in the example above, but how much higher? Have a guess. The answer is given shortly and may surprise you.

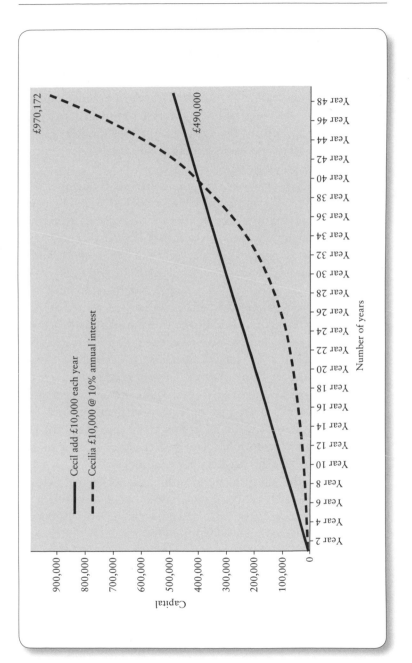

£970,172

£490,000

Capital

900,000
800,000
700,000
600,000
500,000
400,000
300,000
200,000
100,000
0

—— Cecil add £10,000 each year

---- Cecilia £10,000 @ 10% annual interest

Year 2
Year 4
Year 6
Year 8
Year 10
Year 12
Year 14
Year 16
Year 18
Year 20
Year 22
Year 24
Year 26
Year 28
Year 30
Year 32
Year 34
Year 36
Year 38
Year 40
Year 42
Year 44
Year 46
Year 48

Number of years

TAKING ADVANTAGE

Would you be happy to let someone take advantage of you? Would you open your door and allow people in to take what they'd like? Financially, this is in fact standard practice and the people on the receiving end are not just unfortunate victims, they actually sign up for the experience. Either the Marquis de Sade's fan club has increased exponentially or there is another reason. What's going on?

Let's recall the power of compound interest. Remember how 10 per cent annual compound interest on just £10,000 could make you a millionaire by the time you retire? The question was posed, how much you would have to pay back if you borrowed that money at a rate of 30 per cent? When I conducted a straw poll from scratch, answers ranged from £30,000 to £40 million. So is the answer in that range? No, in fact you would have to pay back about £3 billion when you retired. Ouch! Anyone agreeing to this would have to be mad, wouldn't they? Now there is a very simple way to check if you are indeed one sandwich short of a full picnic. Check what percentage annual interest rate you are being charged on your credit card. Ten per cent? Or is it nearer 20 per cent or even the quoted 30 per cent? Whatever it is, if you are not clearing your debts, chances are you are being devoured, at least financially speaking. Are you really comfortable with that? And if so, do you at least understand why your choices are keeping you poor?

Those in the unfortunate position of not being able to obtain a credit card and resorting to doorstep lenders might be paying 100 per cent or, in extreme cases, maybe over 1,000 per cent if it's a loan shark. Or why not go for a 'payday' loan, some providers of which charge more than 4,000 per cent. Most loan sharks would be blushing at charging that rate of interest. That's not 'Ouch!' It's financial torture. Taxi for Mr de Sade!

So why do so many of us agree to these extortionate rates of interest and what can we do about it? Well, if you are starving to death there could be an argument for it. Sometimes paying interest within our Fiat money system is pretty much impossible to avoid and it does depend on individual circumstances. Also few people have the means to buy a house outright and therefore mortgage interest repayments are part and parcel of the deal. Mortgage literally means 'death pledge'. Fortunately mortgage rates are lower than many other forms of loan but you will still end up paying multiples of the original amount borrowed over 25 years. Or how about returning to Roman times when interest rates were restricted, to a maximum of 12 per cent? Now that would be radical, but don't hold your breath ... the beast needs feeding.

Most other loans fall under the want category as opposed to need. Adam Smith argued it didn't make sense to borrow money purely for consumption, it only made sense if the borrower could get a higher return than the interest being paid on the loan. Short-term mentality and modern marketing techniques (i.e. blatantly obscuring the reality) encourage many to succumb to the 'have it now, pay later' disease, but at what cost? Maybe some free money would solve the problem ...

THE STUPIDITY TAX

You are given two choices:

- Pay £2 every day for 50 years and get nothing in return.
- Pay £2 every day for 50 years and get £1 million.

Only the eccentric rich, retarded or outrageously altruistic are going to agree to option one. What if the question was rephrased as follows.

- Pay £2 every day for 50 years and there is a 1 in 64 chance you get £1 million.
- Pay £2 every day for 50 years and get £1 million.

This makes the first option slightly more appealing than in the initial example (at least there is a small chance you may receive the £1 million) but it's still appalling odds and why would you bother if there was an option to definitely receive the money? Wouldn't this be stupidity? Or is it just a tax on stupidity, otherwise known as the National Lottery.

Perhaps a fairer and more appropriate name would be the 'Tax on hope' or given the gambling buzz many people get out of playing, the 'Tax on Dope(amine)' – one of the chemicals of pleasure released within the brain often associated with betting.

In fact, if you really drill down into the subject, it turns out to be a 'tax on anticipation'. Hans Breiter at Harvard Medical School compared the brain scan of someone anticipating a monetary reward with that of a cocaine addict expecting a line. It turned out to be a difficult spot the difference competition.

Back to the maths. To win £1 million on the National Lottery your odds are a measly 2,330,635 to 1. In short, it's very, very unlikely to happen. If you were to bet £2 every day for 50 years, after spending £36,500 (= £2 × 365 × 50) your chances of winning are still only 1 in 64. Obviously better than 2.3 million to 1 but still a long shot given the initial investment. Would you put £36,000 of your money on a horse with odds of 64 to 1? Thought not.

What would happen if instead of playing the Lottery, your £2 bets were to be invested at a rate of 10 per cent per year? In 50 years your money would be worth a cool £1 million. Once again, compound interest has converted £36,500 into £1 million over the time frame. Its option two delivered on a plate.

This example raises many issues concerning our approach to and understanding of money. The Lottery appeals because we crave rewards (that's the brain drugs as much as the actual money) – waiting 50 years doesn't quite satisfy our short-term desires. The image of immediate wealth, or at least the possibility of it, overrides the obvious rationality provided by the mathematics. Get rich slow clearly doesn't appeal as much as get rich quick but the example might at least make you stop and think for a second about how you use your money.

Just as an aside, the original British Lottery was abolished in 1826 after being described as 'radically vicious'. It's sometimes described as a tax on the poor. If you accept that by purchasing a lottery ticket you are involved in a monetary transaction to enjoy the warm temporary feeling of anticipation, not the actual winning, you are in safe territory. Of course, if you do win the jackpot, you weren't that stupid.

More on investment psychology in Chapters 3 and 7 but it's not just the Lottery that one could describe as radically vicious ...

CHEQUEBOOK VANDALISM

Where has all the money gone? One minute we are drowning in the stuff and the next it looks like there is none left. To understand the process we need to wrestle with those woolly mammoths again and the term 'leverage'.

Leverage basically means borrowing. Anyone taking out a mortgage to pay for a house is using money borrowed from the bank to pay for it. A deposit of, say, 10 per cent is offered and the bank lends you the other 90 per cent (well, they used to before they lost it all).

Say you want to buy a house for £100,000 and have a £10,000 deposit. The bank lends you the balance of £90,000. You have borrowed or leveraged nine times your original amount. Now assume house prices rise by 10 per cent in a year and your house is now worth £110,000. You haven't made just 10 per cent; you have in fact doubled your money. You have made £10,000 profit (ignoring costs) on your initial deposit of £10,000. A 100 per cent return in a year. Great! Being highly leveraged in a rising market is very profitable. Or put more succinctly, 'genius is leverage in a bull market'. More bull comes in Chapter 6.

But leverage also works in reverse. Now assume the house dropped in price in the first year by 10 per cent meaning it is only worth £90,000. But you still owe the bank the original loan of £90,000 which means your £10,000 is now worth 100 per cent less, i.e. a big fat zero. Leverage can therefore be just as dangerous as it is beneficial. The £10,000 deposit has disappeared. But where did it go? Well, in this case one could argue it went to the original seller as you probably overpaid for the house. It hasn't disappeared as such, it's just you don't have it anymore and someone else does.

All that explains so far is that we have winners and losers. But let's focus on the change in price. The value of woolly mammoths changed considerably over time depending on circumstances and perceptions. It's exactly the same with other more hair-free and less mobile assets such as housing.

Taking a more extreme example, assume you had purchased the house for £100,000 and you were able to sell it a few years later for £1 million (happy days). Because it has sold for £1 million the market assumes that not only your house is worth a million but the value of all other houses has changed proportionately. This is true only in perception because if everyone wanted to sell their house the next day there would be massive oversupply, prices would crash and therefore the desired price would no longer be achievable. Therefore some wealth is illusory.

This perceived increase in price allows other homeowners to go to a bank and ask to borrow money against the new increased value of their homes (mortgage equity withdrawal). So a homeowner who paid £100,000 but has a house worth £1 million – according to the current market perception – could request a loan of, say, £800,000 from the bank and use the house as collateral, the 'guarantee' the bank will get its money back. Assume this is agreed. The bank isn't giving you £800,000 in currency, it's issuing new money as debt via a loan and it is only able to create this new money because everyone agrees at that moment in time that the house is worth £1 million and there is a promise from the borrower to repay it at some point in the future. As we have seen the bank is able to create money in the form of loans so this can be repeated many times.

Now following some bad news (say the land is found to be somewhat radioactive), everyone loses confidence and the perceived value of the house changes. No one wants to buy and the house is now valued at £100,000 again. The homeowner now owes the £800,000 to the bank but decides as the house is only worth £100,000 they would rather just hand over the keys and declare themselves bankrupt rather than be in so much debt. This loan has now turned bad and it has obvious implications for the bank. If the promise to repay is broken, the stream of money they thought they had coming to them no longer exists and the asset (i.e. the house) isn't worth what they said it was on their books. The bank is leveraged which means this takes a disproportionate toll on its reserves. If this happens many times over, who has the headache?

> ❝ *If you owe the bank $100, that's your problem. If you owe the bank $100 million, that's the bank's problem.* ❞ **John Paul Getty**

So vandalism (and we haven't yet touched on the fraudulent aspects) can be caused by lending too much chequebook money (commercial bank loans) against bad risk and overinflated assets. If this was the only point then the scale of the problem would be much smaller. The fundamental issue was that the bankers also bent the rules. This inherently unstable system is far from perfect, as we have seen, but should have one saving grace; it theoretically puts a maximum limit on how much chequebook money is allowed to enter the system.

By introducing complex securitised products (the financial practice of pooling various types of contractual debt and selling it on) the banks were able to 'remove' loans from their books. Through this and other practices (assisted by the change to modern reserve ratio variants) the loan to deposit ratios at some banks exceeded 100 per cent. Thus any possible mathematical limit of money creation was removed, effectively creating an inverted pyramid of 'limitless' money. Northern Rock, for example, had a loan to deposit ratio of 322 per cent when it went pop. And just like any pyramid scheme it was mathematically doomed by the exponential factor. This was the ultimate in chequebook vandalism. For those wanting more detail I recommend reading Greg Pytel's piece entitled *The Largest Heist in History* and *Where Does Money Come from?* by Josh Ryan-Collins et al.

That's the maths out of the way but the motivation fuelling it was a lack of short-term consequences. Who cares about what happens next year as long as the multi-million pound bonus comes in to land this year?

As has well been documented, short-term bonuses encourage excessive risk-taking but now capitalism, it seems, has turned communist – even failure is rewarded.

66 *You might as well give Lord Cardigan a bonus for the charge of the Light Brigade.* 99 **Boris Johnson**

Banksy: chequebook vandalism 2001

Of course, overcook the chequebook vandalism pot and you may find yourself on the receiving end of some physical vandalism, and it may not be the expensive Banksy you were hoping for:

> 66 *Vandals target Sir Fred Goodwin's house and car.* 99 **Guardian**

~~Sir Fred~~ Mr Goodwin's real problem is that he didn't listen to the advice of John Maynard Keynes at the beginning of this chapter. The ruination of RBS was not conventional enough. If you are going to be a vandal do it anonymously. Even the most 'uneducated' Bristol-born graffiti artist knows that.

Before getting too carried away with the 'bash a banker' ritual it is highly likely, yet an unpalatable truth, that put in the same circumstances many people would have acted in a similar manner. We are often more a victim of circumstance and our cerebral nuances than we ever care to believe, as we will see in Chapter 3. But before we get to your own particular foibles, there is a little more bashing to do and a decision to make. Which pill is it going to be?

CHAPTER 2

Paralytically incorrect

Wake up to your reality

*None are more enslaved than those who
falsely believe they are free* GOETHE

*Of all the contrivances for cheating the labouring classes
of mankind, none has been more effective than that which
deludes them with paper money* DANIEL WEBSTER

PARALYTICALLY INCORRECT

Definition: A consequence of heavy inebriation whereby a gentleman discards his usually tolerant, easy-going views in favour of a more robust manifesto.

WORKING OUT WHAT IS GOING on whilst in the above state would be a challenge for anyone, or put another way, 'in the land of the legless the one legged man is king'.

Many of us, whilst not actually inebriated have, when it comes to money, allowed ourselves to enter a similarly induced *state of paralysis where our ability to function physically, mentally or socially is markedly restricted* – this is the definition of paralytic. We are not paralytically incorrect, we are just incorrect and paralytic.

We don't seem to care how the system works, we use perceived complexity as an excuse not to learn and never question why we are not taught the basics of how the system operates despite being at the sharp end of the consequences. Many of us not only know few of the rules, we don't even know the game that is being played out in front of us. It's time to wake up, and just like the gentleman drunk, we need to adopt a more robust manifesto.

FOLLOW THE WHITE RABBIT

> ❝ *It's human nature to reject what is true but unpleasant, and embrace what is false but comforting.* ❞ **H. L. Mencken**

In the film, *The Matrix*, life is just an elaborate facade, a complex simulation that placates us whilst in reality we are born into a pod where our life-essence is tapped like a battery to fuel a parasitical race of machines. That was a brilliant work of fiction but then so is our current monetary system so it seems eminently appropriate to compare the two. Swop the word 'Matrix' with 'the banking system' and the parallels are all too apparent.

The banking system is all around you. It dominates the world you live in, and in many respects, how you live it. Just like nearly everyone else within it, you are being 'farmed'. Plugged into you and draining you of valuable resources it exploits your ignorance for its own gain whilst you are blissfully unaware of the fact. You have known little else and have never been educated in how it operates so not only can't you explain it, you do not even question it. Insidious; it operates in an inconspicuous and seemingly harmless manner but to grave effect. You are blind to the truth and that truth is beyond your imagination. You are imprisoned inside an artificial reality, a form of bondage, with alas, no hard limits. Or as Morpheus put it '*a prison for your mind.*'

Source: www.marriedtothesea.com

Ignorance is bliss – except when it hurts.

Just like Neo in the film, you too have a choice to make. Do you want to continue believing nothing is wrong and embrace your artificially generated financial reality or do you want to question it and then see how deep the rabbit hole goes? The blue pill is ignorance, the red pill enlightenment. Which is it going to be?

Well, one doesn't really have to drop a coloured disco biscuit to work out there is something fundamentally flawed within the financial system. Just watch *Inside Job*, the award-winning documentary by Charles Ferguson. Or as Nassim Taleb put it: '*Banks have hijacked society... and taken over the government.*'

This documentary is an exposé of the self-interest, manipulation and incompetence that can happen within a system. But let's not pretend this is anything new:

> 66 *We hang the petty thieves and appoint the great ones to public office.* 99 **Aesop, Greek slave and fable author (620–560 BC)**

Of course, as well as commenting on the manipulation, we might want to go one step further and question whether the whole system itself is flawed.

> 66 *Banking is a system that runs on make-believe and survives on ignorance.* 99 **Oliver Huitson**

Welcome to the Money Matrix. You may not know it but the 'good' news is – you are already living the dream. It's just it may not be the one you think it is.

FOR RICHER, FOR POORER

Hooray, we are all getting richer. Or are we? There is no doubt that in the West, compared to previous generations, we have far more toys to play with and numerous more home comforts but this, as many might suspect, isn't quite the whole picture. If you take house prices as a percentage of wages, tuition fees if you have graduate aspirations, and the fact your pension may have disappeared, it is no longer clear that being 'richer' is actually the case. What is indisputable is that the gap between the wealthy and the rest has grown substantially – especially in the US.

Source: www.occupygeorge.com

Or as Jeremy Grantham, chief investment strategist at GMO states, '*The richest 400 people have assets equal to the poorest 140 million. If that doesn't disturb you, you have a wallet for a heart.*'

But how and why did this happen? Philip Coggan, in his book *Paper Promises*, is not alone in fingering the expansion of the money supply as the main reason. It was Adair Turner who highlighted that the finance sector has four roles:

1   Payment services (inc. warehousing).

2   Insurance.

3   Futures market in foreign exchange (FX), interest rates and commodities (generic term for goods).

4   Channelling funds from savers to borrowers.

Coggan argues that the first two roles do not generate huge profits but the last two are where the big money lies, and that these profit centres have expanded dramatically following the expansion of the money supply over the last 40 years.

One of the consequences of constantly expanding the money supply is an increase in asset prices. Coggan points out that money can be viewed as an eternal battle between borrowers and lenders. Under Fiat money conditions, borrowers benefit at the expense of the savers. So, for example, if you invested in housing at the right time you became better off than those that didn't (at least on paper).

However, expanding the money supply certainly benefits one sector in particular, the finance industry, as the more 'money' there is sloshing around in the system, the higher the returns due to more transaction fees, performance fees and interest charges. And let's not forget, as we have seen, those who receive money first get the most benefit. Loosening of caps on the amount of leverage banks and financial institutions were allowed was the best gift of all. *'The banking system used to be described as a 3–6–3 model: borrow money at 3 per cent, lend it at 6 per cent and be on the golf course for 3 pm.'*

At least under the above 'rule' the margins were low, although the more astute may be asking why the interest is even charged in the first place. The theory goes that the lender is taking a risk and therefore should be remunerated. To be perfectly candid and quite frank it's not that outrageous, depending on the rate charged. There are costs and risks involved and the banking system does provide a service.

However, over time the paying of interest and/or fees is in effect transferring wealth from one group to another one. Like the exponential function, the longer the time period and the more interest that is paid, the more the wealth will be polarised. But as the finance industry is an enabler as opposed to a producer one could argue it's feeding itself to the detriment of others. According to Chris Martenson, US banking profits represented about 4 per cent of the economy in the 1940s and at its peak in 2007 it represented 40 per cent.

    ❝ *Why on earth should finance be the biggest and most highly paid industry when it's just a utility, like* *sewage or gas? It is like a cancer that is growing to infinite size until it takes over the entire body.* **99** **Paul Woolley**

Or to put it more acerbically:

66 *Give a man a gun and he can rob a bank. Give a man a bank and he can rob the world.* **99** **Anon**

Give the man a bank *and* a gun and we used to get an even more startling outcome before the shame gene mutated, as John Plender in the *FT* notes: 'When Lazard Brothers, the London arm of the Lazard banking empire, was brought to its knees by a rogue trader in 1931, the miscreant made a confession and shot himself.'

Image from the back of a US dollar bill. Banking: the original and best pyramid scheme?

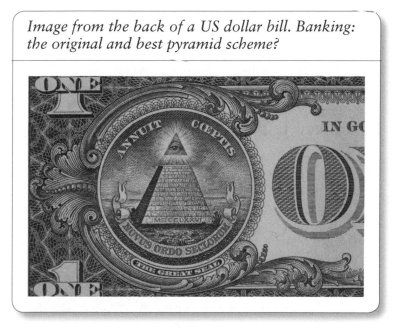

If there is one good thing to emerge out of the financial crisis it is that many more people have a better understanding of how the system works, i.e. for itself.

> ❝ *Bankers focus on two issues: heading off restrictions on their operations and ensuring they can carry on paying themselves huge sums of money.* ❞ **Michael Skapinker**, *Financial Times*.

So there you have it. You have the privilege of paying interest to a private organisation, mostly on money that it never had to begin with. Alles klar?

'*It does not make sense*' isn't just a 'Chewbacca defence'. There is, however, a light at the end of the tunnel. It's not a scene from *Poltergeist*, it is, in fact, the oncoming gravy train.

DE-RAILING THE GRAVY TRAIN

It could be said **the banking system is a larceny, wrapped in a mystery inside an anathema.** Theft, opaqueness and loathing all rolled into one – sounds like a thriller. Or maybe it's simply a tragedy and not necessarily all Greek.

> ❝ *While the incompetent may elicit our scorn, they do not merit our moral indignation. That is reserved for the unscrupulous.* ❞ **Kurt Cobb**

Although a popular pastime and not entirely inaccurate, blaming the bankers is a lazy argument. Bankers are human and humans will extract as much as any particular system affords. The problem runs deeper through undisciplined 'paper' currency and the underlying system itself.

> ❝ *That banks get ever bigger, that they routinely hand out multi-million dollar bonuses, and that they frequently get bailed out, is not a result of the greed of the bankers ... but is integral to the fiat money system.* ❞ **Detlev Schlichter**

The Money Matrix is made up of three parts, which are rarely questioned. Central banks, fractional reserve banking (or the modern variation of it) and Fiat currency. It's the usual suspects, the profligate, the illusionary and the infinite and they are all looking as if they are guilty as charged.

So what are the alternatives? It is not within the scope of this book to explicitly detail them all but options exist and surely can't be any worse than what we already have? 'What would Jesus do?' (see his answer overleaf). We can, however, take a moment to debunk three myths surrounding the current system.

Banking myth 1

We need central banks to be a lender of last resort to stop commercial banks from going bust in times of crisis.

Well, the world still functioned before the central banks arrived. Sure, banks went bust but this isn't necessarily as bad as many bankers would have you believe. As long as depositors' money is safeguarded (which it can be) making banks accountable, as opposed to just responsible, for their lending is generally a good idea.

      66 *Risk-bearing is a wonderful mechanism for regulating human decision making.* 99 **Ron Paul, End The Fed**

A more renowned figure and Austrian School economist, F. A. Hayek leaves out the vernacular but when it comes to central banking stated: '*I doubt whether it has ever done any good except to the rulers and their favourites.*'

Advocates of 'free banking' see central banks as the problem not the solution. Given central banks around the world are generally responsible for regulating the commercial banks, have massively inflated their balance sheets, printed enormous amounts of Fiat currency, created housing bubbles by leaving rates too low, and have demonstrated as much accuracy with their inflation targeting as a blind man with Parkinson's disease trying to hit a bull's-eye on a galloping antelope, one starts to see why they might be thinking that.

What is worse than banks failing? We have now found out; banks not failing. The money still disappears, it's just out of the back door instead of the front.

Banking myth 2

Without a 'fractional reserve system' the sky would fall in.

As we saw in Chapter 1 the whole system of fractional reserve banking (FRB) and its modern variant is inherently unstable. If everyone wants their money back at the same time it collapses. Would you design a bus that automatically crashed if a quarter of the passengers got off? And which other business in the land is allowed to trade whilst permanently insolvent? When it comes to our system of money is this really the best we can come up with? Spanish economist Jesus Huerta de Soto, in his 812-page epic *Money, Bank Credit and Economic Cycles* (the insomniac's favourite), argues for a 100 per cent reserve requirement as an antidote. As usual not everyone agrees that is the solution but as fractional reserve banking appears to be as much a source of *in*stability as stability, at least it looks like the sky is in for some double jeopardy.

But to really tip the scales we need some added irresponsibility from the government and central banks. Roll the presses …

Banking myth 3

Fiat currency is a good idea.

Never in the history of humankind has limitless paper currency been a good idea but obviously this time it's different! The Chinese tried it in the 9th century – epic fail, so did the

French via John Law in the 18th century – epic fail, and well before that the Romans and the Greeks had a debasement extravaganza leading to ... epic empire fail. If financial history teaches us one thing it is that unsound currency ends badly.

As Ludwig von Mises put it:

> ❝ the crisis should come sooner as a result of voluntary abandonment of further credit expansion, or later as a final and total catastrophe. ❞

There have been times when we have existed with sound (or non-elastic) currency. In England, between 1694 and 1894, the price of a Hackney carriage trip didn't alter in price. That's 200 years of sound money and no inflation (at least not in taxi rides). This was because the paper pound was put on a gold standard during which we coincidently experienced the industrial revolution. Every system has its flaws (including gold standards) but none more so than unlimited paper currency. Our Fiat money system is a collapse waiting to happen.

Just like the film version, this Money Matrix is accepted just because it's there and you have known little else. What's more, Jesus thinks it is interfering with your freedom. Jesus Huerta de Soto said, 'The main challenge to face both professional economists and lovers of freedom in this new century will be to use all of their intellectual might to oppose the institution of the central bank and the privilege private bankers now enjoy.'

There is no perfect system but the one we have looks like it needs a ride with a wise guy over the Austrian border. Some would argue that if you want change you can do one of three things. Vote, revolt or halt:

● **Vote:** requires a candidate who understands the system, is willing to change it and after being elected is able to avoid assassination prior to doing so. Given most politicos are part of the problem, voting in more of the same looks like a fruitless strategy. However, many grass roots initiatives are underway in several countries such as 'Positive Money' in the UK.

- **Revolt:** involves severe disruption and social unrest. It's coming anyway* so why not get in early and avoid the rush?

- **Halt:** means extricating yourself and many others from the system (but have you tried living in the modern world without a bank account?).

Choose your poison, as they say.

> 66 *People are beginning to get angry – but not nearly enough!* 99 **Prof. Herman Daly, former senior World Bank economist,** *Four Horsemen*

Is there a chance the gravy train might just derail itself without everyone getting too hot under the collar? If chaos theory converges with a loss of confidence there could be a lot of gravy spilt and it might not need organising. To explain that last sentence we are going to jump into someone else's sandpit.

Imagine creating a pile of sand by dropping single grains, one at a time, onto a table. Once a pile is formed the next grain is added and you witness an avalanche in the sand. You might ask yourself two questions at this point. Is there a typical number of grains required before there is a collapse and was the additional grain of sand the reason the avalanche occurred?

Bak, Tang and Weisenfeld decided to investigate this avalanche phenomenon creating a computer program to mimic the behaviour of sand under these conditions. After a huge number of tests they discovered there was in fact no typical number of grains required to start an avalanche. Further tests were then undertaken to try to understand what was happening.

---

* Nicholas Taleb was asked on *Newsnight* by Jeremy Paxman whether the riots in Athens were a black swan event. He replied: '… rather the real black swan event is that more people are not rioting elsewhere.' 15 June, 2011. NB: It didn't take long for him to be proved prescient.

By looking down from above the pile and using the computer to colour steeper areas in red and the more stable, flatter areas in green they were able to see how each pile developed.

As the sand pile grew in size more red areas (ready to collapse) appeared. These would appear initially as individual spots of colour which would then grow in size as more grains were added. Isolated red spots may have limited repercussions if hit by a single grain but when red areas come to dominate the pile, the consequences of the next grain become *'fiendishly unpredictable'*.

John Mauldin has used this chaos theory thinking from Mark Buchanan's book *Ubiquity* and then applied it to markets by explaining the 'fingers of instability' concept. He states:

> 'It may trigger only a few tumblings, or it might instead set off a cataclysmic chain reaction involving millions. This is referred to as being in a critical state. After the pile evolves into a critical state, many grains link up into "fingers of instability" of all possible lengths. While many are short, others slice through the pile from one end to the other. So a chain reaction triggered by a single grain might lead to an avalanche of any size. What makes one avalanche much larger than another depends on the perpetually unstable organisation of the critical state. And it isn't the last grain of sand that causes the pile to collapse but the farthest reason – the underlying instability of the system.'

Furthermore he adds:

> 'The greatest events may have no special or exceptional causes.'

So is our financial system in a critical state? Well one thing's for sure you won't find out by just looking at it.

> **❝** *Complex systems that have artificially suppressed volatility tend to become extremely fragile, while at the same time exhibiting no visible risks.* **❞ Nassim Nicholas Taleb and Mark Blyth**

What we do know is that by attempting to avoid minor problems we create major ones. Due to previous attempts to stop the pile collapsing, by pumping the system full of Fiat money and dropping interest rates to near zero, the fingers have grown in length and now really do slice through the financial system from one end to the other. So when the avalanche does happen it's probably going to be a doozy.

You don't need to understand how the complexities of the financial system work (few do, including the experts) but realise this. When you increase the scale of any complex system you do not limit risk but increase it. And what is worse is that risk does not increase in a linear fashion but exponentially (it's our old friend again). Look how large 'the pile' has become and then ask yourself one question. Is this stability or instability?

> 66 *By 2007, the international financial system was trading derivatives* valued at one quadrillion dollars per year. This is ten times the total worth, adjusted for inflation, of all products made by the world's manufacturing industries over the last century.* 99 **Ian Stewart, *The Guardian***

There was a reason that Warren Buffett wrote in 2002: '*In my view, derivatives are financial weapons of mass destruction … the troubles of one could quickly infect the others.*'

But hey, '**What could possibly go wrong?**' Using the bankruptcy of MF Global as an example, Kurt Cobb suggests that the '*world's financial system may be moving headlong into a collision of incompetence with unscrupulousness.*' MF Global allegedly dipped into their clients' accounts to try to save itself prior to collapse. Cobb states:

---

* A derivative is a contract (security) between two or more parties whose value is derived from the price of the underlying asset. They are generally used as an instrument to hedge risk (e.g. Foreign Currency exchange). The problem is that the derivative itself is not an asset but people often assume it has the same qualities. It does not.

'If authorities do everything right, but investors believe they
can no longer trust their brokers and banks not to steal their
assets, the competence of the authorities in monetary and
fiscal policy will simply not matter. And, if investors should
simultaneously lose faith in the ability of authorities to
handle the rolling financial crisis we should be prepared for a
wipeout.'

So have incompetence, greed and corruption within the system
already sown the seeds of its own destruction? And have the
bank bailouts, by creating one rule for some and not for others,
added an additional layer of distrust? Having nowhere left to
trust being the trigger that inadvertently derails the gravy train?

Remember, money deposited by you in a bank legally
belongs to the bank but is registered as a liability. It's like lending
a friend some money and receiving an IOU in exchange. It is
no longer owned by the saver and is now only their asset. It
only requires a small percentage of people to say, *I don't trust
you, could I have my money back, please?'* and then everyone is
heading for the exit at the same time. Surely not, that would be
herding, and we'll see in Chapter 3 that no one gets involved in
that sort of behaviour ...

According to an article in *Der Speigel* it's already happened
in Greece:

'At the start of 2010, savings and time deposits held by private
households in Greece totalled €237.7 billion – by the end of
2011, they had fallen by €49 billion. Since then, the decline
has been gaining momentum.'

Who is brave enough to claim Euro contagion cannot occur
especially when there is no deposit insurance scheme? But bank
runs are infrequent and less likely (but still eminently possible)
where the government has offered depositors a guarantee, as is
the case in the UK with an £85,000 per account (per separate
institution) defensive carrot – to alleviate the 'minor inconvenience' that if a bank goes bust you may not be entitled to your

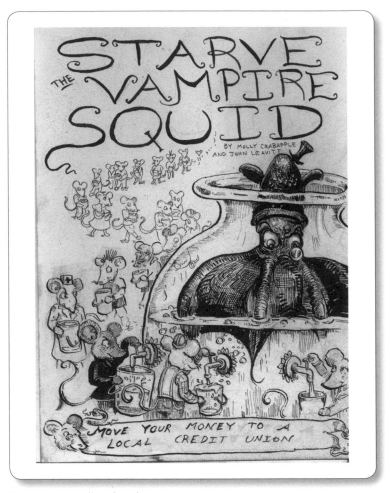

Source: www.mollycrabapple.com

money back. After all, as you now know they can just create it by typing £85,000 onto a computer screen in order to give it back to you – it's just that at that point it won't buy what it used to (there's that back door again).

But it doesn't require a bank run or the general public to start a systemic collapse. That could happen when insiders within the system lose faith in it or the rogue trader is actually a rogue algorithm (see Chapter 6). Will we have a loss of faith converging with the overextended fingers of instability within the markets to create the mother of all fallouts? I have no idea whether any of the above will come to pass or which 'grain of sand' could trigger it, but it looks perfectly feasible, and if it does escalate a lot of 'gravy' is going overboard. The question is, what are you going to do? Sit there like a startled bunny or act in advance? Rabbit stew it is, then. If you don't want to be on the menu then a few suggestions on how to avoid being the main ingredient will be covered in Chapters 7 and 8.

If and when the gravy has been spilt perhaps the questioning of the whole Money Matrix will start in earnest. This would not be that surprising as we reinvent our monetary system every so often anyway. Maybe this time rather than a quick tinker we can give it a proper overhaul? The current one is kaput.

At least one person thinks there is about to be a gravy shortage:

> *Finance has had its great 30 years. We have had many periods in history when the financial types have been in charge but then periods where people who produce real goods are in charge. Well, we are shifting again from the financial types to the producers of real goods.* **Jim Rogers**

A BIT OF A KERFUFFLE

> *Sometimes people don't want to hear the truth because they don't want their illusions destroyed.* **Friedrich Nietzsche**

Remember in Chapter 1 we saw how money is created from effectively nothing? And Voltaire's observation that all paper money returns to its intrinsic value – zero. There is a pattern of events that is playing out before your eyes. One that has occurred many times before.

In order to understand what is happening you may even have to fundamentally change your belief system. As we will see in Chapter 7, the human brain tends to extrapolate in a linear fashion. The problem is that we a have moved from a benign to a distinctly interesting environment.

And it may be more than just a problem we face, it may be a predicament. This difference was aptly coined by Chris Martenson who explains problems have solutions, predicaments have outcomes. In short, it looks like we are in a predicament and there's going to be a bit of a kerfuffle.

Paper money is so ingrained in our psyche that we need to change our belief system, it's only there as medium to pay for goods that are actually useful. It's in effect a paper representation of our blood, sweat and tears.

> 'Money needs to still retain a contractual value. Under the present system of Fiat money, there is quite literally no contract whatsoever and the value of money in exchange rests in its entirety on the delusion that there is an underlying contract. Such a system has huge risk, because if ever there comes a point where individuals demand that the contract they believe to be there is fulfilled, they will find that there is nothing there at all.' **Cynicuseconomicus**

As we have seen, paper currencies used to be backed by gold, then they were devalued to a smaller percentage of gold and eventually became backed by nothing except a promise. This devaluation has not only continued over time but also the rate of devaluation has increased substantially. 'Paper money', especially in the US and UK, is being created at an unprecedented rate in the modern era and enjoying the consequences is going to be your privilege.

> ❝ *May you live in interesting times.* ❞
> **Chinese curse**

The great moderation has become the great correction (or is that the greater depression?) and the endgame may be Western currency destruction. It is not guaranteed but unless we change tack it is the most likely outcome. The point is illustrated by Schlichter in his book, *Paper Money Collapse*. The elasticity of money may sound like an abstract concept but it's actually easily understood with a little common sense. One theory (not Schlichter's, I hasten to add) states that currency should be issued at a rate that is supposed to match the growth in goods and services that are exchanged. If we are tied to a fixed amount of money then as growth in goods and trade expands, in extreme circumstances, the money system *may* struggle to keep up. Alternatively, if there is no restriction, we end up with a paper tiger à la Zimbabwe, and it can lose all its value. As in life, it's good to have some standards.

Gold may or may not work as a 'new' global currency – but its non-elasticity is why it is a good measuring standard for currencies. The opposite of this non-elastic money is totally elastic money and that's what we have now. Just 'print' whatever you want to without restriction and at no cost. Elastic money is like elastic in knickers. You can have a lot of fun stretching it a long way but eventually it snaps and, just like the lingerie version, once it does, you are going to be severely embarrassed when it's limply hanging around your ankles. It's now worthless but fiddling with it proved irresistible:

> 66 *Men would first have to be capable of unlimited self-discipline to resist any temptation to increase money arbitrarily, even if their very existence ... were at stake.* 99 **Adolph Wagner, 1868**

I mentioned in the Introduction that our journey starts by following the money and 'pulling its pants down'. Apparently I needn't have bothered – as you can see the authorities will ensure that they end up in that position regardless.

Just like a set of lingerie obsessives the allegiance that is central bankers and politicians know that all the stretching they are doing isn't going to end well but they just can't help themselves. They don't want to annihilate their currency but the time to behave responsibly never arrives. The alternative is ugly, unpopular *and* they get fingered for it. So instead of a resolution we get postponement and eventually *much more pain*. Genius.

But hold on; are we in danger of making a false prediction?

> 66 *Those who have knowledge don't predict. Those who predict don't have knowledge.* 99 **Lao Tzu**

Well, Tzu, I doff my cap to your infinite wisdom and you are absolutely spot on but that doesn't mean you shouldn't look where you are going. To use a simple driving analogy, there is only one problem with not ever looking forward; by doing so you are generally looking in the rear view mirror. If you do that for too long you tend to end up in a head-on crash. But hey, this particular crash isn't a problem, it only involves a bit of worthless paper.

> 66 *Whether ancient or modern ... each nation descends pretty much the same slippery slope, expanding government to address perceived needs, accumulating too much debt, and then repudiating its obligations by destroying its currency.* 99 **James Turk**

So it all works fine as long as everyone can suspend their disbelief in the face of reality. Ignorance is no longer an excuse. We need to protect our hard earned from the *potential* onslaught.

> 66 *You need a glass of 'harden the f**k up', mate.* 99 **'Chopper'**

The only person you can trust is yourself. Time for some more fighting talk ...

CHAPTER 3

Fighting instincts

Understanding human behaviour and risk

We have met the enemy ... and he is us POGO

If the human brain were so simple that we could understand it, we would be so simple that we couldn't EMERSON M. PUGH

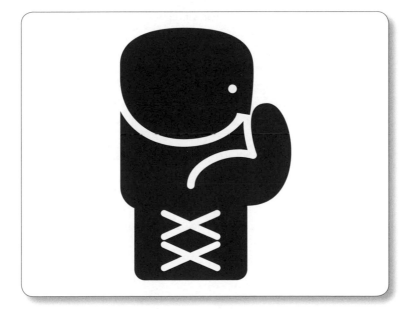

FIGHT, FLIGHT AND BLIGHT

If you don't want to end up as 'bunny roadkill' should the gravy train derail, it'd be sensible to take some proactive action. Trouble is, there is just one small *matter* to overcome, it's the lesser spotted *grey* variety and it belongs to you. The human brain is the most exceptional piece of biological engineering ever to roam the planet. Developed over millions of years, we marvel at its unparalleled capability. Well, now you can stop marvelling and start cursing, because when it comes to deciding what to do with your money it may be working more against you than for you. The human brain has developed to deal with different environments and situations over the millennia, most of which focused on which predators to avoid until a Baldrick-like cunning plan had been devised. Not much time was spent pondering which incomprehensible and totally inappropriate financial investments to avoid. And whilst we have an enviable reputation for being highly adaptable, many of the inherent reactions we have developed are hardwired into our systems. So before even thinking about what to do with our money or what's the best strategy to adopt we first must understand how our emotions and instincts affect our decision-making ability. If we can recognise our weaknesses we have the chance to avoid them, or at least try to be more aware of their impact.

Ever been in two minds about something? This isn't a temporary state of indecision but a physical reality when it comes to your brain. It appears to be made up of two separate systems based on emotion and rationality. System 1 is instinct and System 2 is reason. Both systems have defining qualities.

System 1: Instinct

- Fast.

- Unconscious.

- Needs few observations.

- 'Saves your bacon.'

System 2: Reason

- Slow.

- Conscious.

- Calculating.

- Saves you looking stupid.

Instinct helps us to stay alive. A rapid, reflex response to fear is essential for survival, however when it comes to investing it's often better to think first and react later. So how much are we really blighted by our own fight or flight system and can our brains weigh the alternatives in a more rational fashion? If you haven't come across it before try this question:

> A bat and ball together cost £1.10. The bat costs £1.00 more than the ball. How much does the ball cost? Decide first and only then check your answer at the bottom of the page.* If you didn't get it correct don't worry, you are in illustrious company. Most people don't, but why?

'OOPS!' INSIDE YOUR HEAD

It appears that our brains are hardwired for 'malfunction' in certain situations. For example, a car is designed to run on the road; put it in a swimming pool and its performance deteriorates slightly. The same is true with humans; a few hundred years of modern living is not going to fully rewire a brain that has developed over a much longer time span.

* £0.05 and the bat £1.05.

A whole field of study has emerged combining neuroscience with 'the dismal science' (economics) to create the imaginatively named neuro-economics. This also goes by the equally imaginative names of behavioural finance/behavioural economics/ behavioural investing, etc. This is an attempt to gain a better understanding of how the brain functions when faced with investment decisions. Unlike the mythical 'homo-economicus' who is defined to be 100 per cent rational, we are blinkered by a variety of cognitive biases. Let's identify some of these before examining their implications.

Processing Errors

These are a disreputable group of cranial laggards who ensure that information is misinterpreted, and decoys, along with the irrelevant, are swallowed whole. Let's meet them.

Framing

The way facts are presented influences how we react to them. Take this example from Massimo Piattelli-Palmarini in his book, *Inevitable Illusions*. Two separate groups of doctors were given the survival rates for a particular operation. Group 1 were told there was a 93 per cent survival rate and the second group told there was a 7 per cent mortality rate. Those are identical statistics but whereas the doctors from Group 1 were enthusiastic to recommend the operation the second group were reluctant.

Actually it gets worse, because not only are we influenced by the presentation as in the above case, we are also affected by how well we can relate to it. For example, Paul Slovac discovered that many people will think a 1 in 100 chance offers a higher risk than 1 per cent even though they mean the same thing. This is because percentages are a more abstract notion and therefore less meaningful from a human perspective. It seems our brains are wired for stories more than for numbers. So you may react differently to the same set of facts, depending on how it's put to you.

Anchoring

Decisions are easily influenced by irrelevant initial values.

EXAMPLE

A supermarket put up a sign above a large display of soup saying *'Limit of 12 per person'*. Shoppers were monitored and the average purchase was seven cans, with no one buying two cans or fewer. When the sign was removed the average purchase was 3.3 cans. The number 12 acted as an anchor point and a subconscious influence doubling the average number of cans purchased per customer.

Anchoring can work in ways that are wholly unexpected. For example, it has been demonstrated that by putting a minimum payment amount on a credit card statement it actually subconsciously encourages people to pay off less per month than when it isn't shown – the stated minimum payment becomes an anchor people react to.

These anchoring type experiments have been repeated many times with similar results and interestingly no participants believed, when asked, that the initial number given had in any way influenced their decision.

A price may appear good value after a drop but if the original anchor price was high it doesn't make the new price cheap. Discount sofas anyone?

Heuristics

Rules of thumb for dealing with complex situations or incomplete information.

EXAMPLE

Price implies quality bias. Researchers have shown that people perceive more expensive wines as tasting better than inexpensive ones. Volunteers in a Californian study were asked to sample and rate different bottles of Cabernet Sauvignon. Unbeknown to the volunteers, the bottles had all been labelled with an incorrect price. Bottles labelled with a higher price were ranked as more enjoyable than lower priced wines, despite the fact that some of the price changes were very dramatic – a $90 bottle passed off as a $10 bottle for example and a $5 bottle upgraded to $45.

Seems like this is a great opportunity for the pretentious and financially challenged to slash the costs at dinner parties, just slap a vintage label on that bottle of vinegar.

The above-mentioned processing errors are only the beginning of our weaknesses, in fact they are probably the least damaging. Let's tuck into some proper cognitive disorder.

Self-Deception

As Abe Lincoln once said, '… *you may fool all of the people some of the time; you can even fool some of the people all of the time; but you can't fool all of the people all of the time.*' He should have finished the sentence with, '*they can do that for themselves, thank you very much.*' When it comes to fooling ourselves we are all at it but in a somewhat inconspicuous manner.

Competency bias

People have an inflated view of their own abilities.

> **EXAMPLE**
>
> In a study conducted by Princeton University, 70 per cent of drivers rated themselves above average!
>
> **NB:** Remember the proverb, confidence is what you feel before you comprehend the situation.

Hindsight bias

'No idea what's going to happen' mysteriously converts into *'I knew it all along'*, post the event.

Self-attribution bias

If a decision was right it was skill, if it was wrong it was bad luck.
NB: Luck plays a bigger role than you think.

Optimism bias

Overestimating the likelihood of positive events and underestimating the likelihood of negative events.

> **EXAMPLE**
>
> College students were asked to rate whether they were more or less likely than other students to experience a range of life events – some positive, some negative. Psychologist Neil Weinstein found that students generally believed the good things were more likely to happen to them, and the bad things less likely compared to their peers.

NB: There is nothing wrong with being optimistic in life but when it comes to investment it is always wise to consider the negative scenarios before taking the plunge. For example, ask yourself, *'How much money could I lose?'* not *'How much money could I gain?'*

Confirmation bias

People seek only information that agrees with their existing beliefs.

EXAMPLE

How many of us only read newspapers that best fit with our own views? We know all newspapers have their own political and social biases, but often we still choose to read those which are a close fit to our beliefs. Time to change that? Or what about reading the foreign press to eliminate the UK bias and get a more rounded view?

A more formal demonstration of this effect was conducted by psychologist, Peter Cathcart Wason in 1960 when he created the 2–4–6 problem. Participants were presented with the sequence 2, 4, 6 and told that the sequence conformed to a particular rule. They were then asked to discover the rule by generating their own three digit sequence and using feedback they received from the experimenter. Every time the participant generated a three digit sequence, the experimenter would indicate whether the sequence conformed to the rule. The participants were told that once they were sure what the rule was they should announce it.

Participants tested only 'positive' examples, i.e. sequences they believed would conform to their rule and confirm their hypothesis. So if they believed the rule is 'numbers increasing by 2', they would say 'Does 8, 10, 12 follow the rule?' The examiners would answer yes. 'Does 15, 17 and 19 follow the rule?', and again the answer would be yes. Once the participant had established enough examples to 'prove' the hypothesis the rule would be announced. 'Is it numbers increasing by two?'

What they did not do was attempt to challenge or falsify their hypotheses by testing sequences that they believed would not fit their rule. This would have proved much more effective. It only takes one example of a negative to prove the rule to be wrong. Wason referred to this phenomenon as confirmation bias, whereby people systematically seek only evidence that confirms their existing views. The rule was not numbers increasing by two but any three numbers in ascending order.

Tip: Play devil's advocate with yourself to see if you are missing something.

Conservative bias

An underreaction to events.

EXAMPLE

You decide to stay invested in the stock market despite witnessing the worst financial crisis in 80 years slowly unfold! *'What's that you're wearing? Smells like failure.'*

Tip: If the situation calls for action don't just stand there, do something.

Know anyone with these afflictions? Many of them have clear influences on investors' behaviour. However, before we start bashing our brains learning the full financial consequences and indulging in the associated avoidance rituals we are going to investigate brain bashing of a different kind.

THE CURIOUS CASE OF PHINEAS GAGE

Phineas Gage's experience in 1848 is the sort that would make even the *Jackass* team reach for their pipe and slippers. Gage worked as a foreman on the Rutland and Burlington railroad, laying track and generally blowing up anything that got in his way. Unfortunately at 4.30 p.m. on 13 September this also included his own brain when he accidently blew a three-foot long metal rod through it. This is how the events were reported in the local paper:

> The iron entered on the side of his face, shattering the upper jaw and passing back of the left eye, and out of the top of the head. The singular circumstance connected with this melancholy affair, that he was alive at two o'clock this afternoon, and in full possession of his reason, and free from pain.
>
> *Free Soil Union*, Ludlow, Vermont

Two months after the involuntary brain mutilation incident Gage was fully healed but not fully cured. The metal rod had landed 30 yards away, but Gage's personality had apparently followed it and gone West. '*Gage was no longer Gage*' were the comments at the time. Much of his emotional capacity had disappeared and it was noted by his physician that Gage now vacillated over decisions, '*devising many plans of future operation, which were no sooner arranged than they were abandoned.*'

Do Gage's post-incident reactions indicate there is a connection between emotion and decision-making ability? And if so, what is it? Let's join the dots with the aid of Lee Alan Dugatkin's concept of 'rational economic man'.

Antonio Damasio in his book, *Descartes' Error* highlights a similar set of symptoms to those of Gage with a patient who had a large brain tumour in his right frontal lobe. Not only was he almost devoid of emotion but whenever he was asked to make a decision that had social consequences he would freeze, incapable of choosing among the range of possible options.

From this work, Damasio concluded that *'Emotion and rational decision making – that is, reason – are not separate phenomena.'*

So it appears we can't make a rational decision without emotion. That's not what most people's understanding of rational is.

PETS 'r' US

Positron emission tomography (PET) and functional magnetic resonance imaging (fMRI) have allowed neuroscientists to reveal a little more about the brain's modus operandi than just setting tasks and collating results. Subjects are hooked up to the machines whilst scientists observe and record their brain activity. This allows an unprecedented glimpse into the workings of the brain as it makes decisions.

Let's return to the first bias we raised, which was framing (the way things are presented influences how we react to them) but this time use a PET/fMRI scan to find out which areas of the brain are active and see what's going on.

Benedetto De Martino of University College London monitored brain activity under the influence of gambling. At the point of making the decision to gamble or not the team found a neural region called the amygdala 'lit up', an area normally associated with fear or negative emotions. Where people were resisting a framing effect two more areas of the brain lit up also – one associated with positive emotions and one relating to decision making. It was almost as if the different areas were trying to have a fight.

This idea of a boxing match between emotion and rationality is easy to relate to, but it seems emotion has a horseshoe in one of its gloves ready to deliver the knockout blow. '*We found everyone showed emotional biases, more or less; no one was totally free of them,*' De Martino said. Four participants knew they were inconsistent in their decision making but reported they 'couldn't help themselves'.

THE PARADOX

If we take Damasio's and De Martino's research at face value it would appear there is a paradox at work. Emotions produce irrational results but *yet emotions are necessary for rational decision making and behaviour.* Is the paradox real or is there something we are missing?

To investigate the phenomenon, let's look at another gambling scenario, the Ultimatum game, where two people are taking part in an economic transaction over a set amount of money. One is the proposer, the other has to react to any offer made and is therefore the responder. In the game only one person controls the money resource, namely the proposer. The game is structured as follows ...

The proposer offers the responder a proportion of the money. If the responder accepts the offer they both get to keep what has been suggested. In the case the offer is rejected then neither of them receives anything.

For example, suppose there is £100 in the pot. The proposer offers the responder £50. If the responder agrees, each player gets £50. But if the responder refuses, they both get nothing.

It is in the best interest of the proposer to offer the smallest amount of money that they believe the responder will accept, thereby allowing the proposer to take as much of the money as possible. If the responder is behaving purely rationally they should accept any offer above zero, as otherwise they get nothing as an alternative.

However, perhaps not surprisingly the results tell a different story. If the offer is not half, or very close to half the money, the responder often rejects it, even though by doing so they end up with nothing. Rational economic reasoning is often overridden by anger and a sense of the offer being unfair. Is this actually irrational, as many have claimed?

It appears that many economic decisions are made within a social context. We care about how we fare economically when compared to others.

This issue of emotions and rational behaviour with respect to cooperation, cheating and punishment has been analysed by numerous neuroscientists. Dominique de Quervain at the University of Zurich proposed that people derive pleasure from enforcing social norms via punishment. The area of the brain associated with reward (that's the dorsal striatum if you're interested) became particularly active when the player committed the act of retribution, and the more severe the punishment for the cheater, the more active the dorsal striatum became on the PET scanner.

What are the hidden benefits to people punishing cheaters even when such enforcement is costly to themselves? The answer appears to lie in that much undervalued character trait called reputation.

Let's return to the Ultimatum game. If losing money was the only possible loss, not taking the offer of the proposer would indeed be irrational, however in real life, by turning down the proposer's offer, a clear message is sent out to others that the responder will not accept unfair offers. Whilst the responder has incurred a short-term loss they have potentially generated a long-term benefit. The gain in reputation may outweigh short-term monetary loss. Their standing in the community and their sense of self-worth are enhanced, all of which have long-term economic, as well as other, consequences. So the irrational may occasionally be deemed rational depending on context.

For example, say your partner gives you a particular scent as they have been away travelling. You may feel that is a thoughtful present and gladly accept it. A number of years later they are still travelling and every time they return with the *same* scent. Whilst you still wear it well, you might now perchance refuse the gift and emotionally 'nurse' it into the bin without explicitly stating why. Your partner looks agog and thinks you are being irrational. From your perspective the decision makes perfect sense as you no longer want to accept gifts where so little thought has been applied and want to ensure this is not repeated (although there's not a cat in hell's chance you are going to tell them the reason if they're too stupid to work it out for themselves).

Scientists such as Robert Frank et al. have argued that in socially complex environments the pursuit of self-interest requires emotions and, what's more, we cannot extract emotions from rational decisions, we can only temper them. This has implications for investors, so let's see what ensues when we inadvertently deploy some of them ...

Fear

Fear is the most powerful emotion when it comes to investing. It can be split into two varieties:

Ambiguity aversion

People hesitate or are fearful in situations where there is uncertainty.

> #### EXAMPLE
>
> Suppose you have two bags, the first containing ten black balls and ten white balls. The second bag contains 20 balls in total but the proportion of black and white balls is unknown. You are now told you will win £100 if the first ball that is selected is a black ball, but which bag will you choose from? Research shows that most people prefer to bet on the bag with a known content of ten white and ten black balls as opposed to a bag with unknown proportions of the two colours. People show a greater fear of the unknown – this is ambiguity aversion.

Loss aversion

Fear of losing money.

> ### EXAMPLE
>
> Shiv and Bacara at Stanford University devised a 20-round gambling game to study the topic. Participants were given $20 to start with. The rules were simple. Participants were invited to risk $1 per round on the toss of a coin. If on a particular round someone chose not to bet they would keep the $1 whereas those that did choose to bet on the heads/tails outcome would either earn $2.50 if they chose correctly, or lose $1 if they called it incorrectly.
>
> From a mathematical perspective there was a 50:50 chance of winning so it made sense to take the risk on every round as the average payout for participating was $1.25 versus only $1 for not participating. In reality people only participated 58 per cent of the time and fear seemed to influence behaviour. *'What we found out is that individuals were reacting emotionally to the outcome of the previous round ... if they lost money, they got scared and had the tendency to fall back and decline to play further.'*

Of course fear isn't the only emotion we have to worry about. Look what happens when we get aroused ...

Lust

Whether this is bad or just plain naughty depends on your perspective but the following experiment certainly fits into the mischievous category.

EXAMPLE

Ariely and Loewenstein wanted to test how people's choices would vary depending on their emotional state at the time. The emotion chosen was lust and in order to recreate this they decided to employ a group of male students at the University of California and ask them to indulge in some private self-gratification whilst answering a series of questions on a laptop computer. There appeared to be no obvious shortage of volunteers or indeed innuendo opportunity. Students were asked to answer first in a 'cold' state and then asked to repeat the experiment in a 'hot' state. 'Hot' meaning 75 per cent aroused.

'Obvious' questions included:

- Is a woman sexy when she's sweating?
- Can you imagine having sex with a 60-year-old woman?
- Would it be fun to tie up your sexual partner?
- Would you slip a woman a drug to increase the chance that she would have sex with you?

The last question somewhat worryingly had the largest increase between cold and hot states. NB. If you think these are twisted you may wish to avoid reading the full list – it gets worse.

The differences between the respondents' answers when aroused and non-aroused were considerable. Morality decreased on average by 15 to 20 percentage points under the aroused state as the men succumbed to the classic north to south 'brain repositioning' process that most women are, alas, all too familiar with. The last of the four questions listed above varied by a mere 420 per cent.

So what does this show apart from the fact male university students have a high libido and need little encouragement to indulge in DIY carnal pleasures? When we are cold (clear headed and rational) we believe we will make the same choices as when we are in a hot (emotionally elevated) situation. The reality is that we don't think the same when emotions are flowing, regardless of whether it's lust, greed, fear or any other state. This difference is sometimes referred to as an **empathy gap**. It has big implications for all of us, as we will find out later. And after lust comes ...

Love

'Just say nope to dope(amine)' is about as effective as employing a group of sugar-starved kids as security guards in a sweetie shop. Dopamine and serotonin are the drugs of pleasure and reward and one way of releasing these is to fall in love. According to Dr Helen Fischer there are three stages of love – lust, romantic love and attachment.

Scientists at University College London led by Dr Andreas Bartels have found that:

> '... feelings of love lead to a suppression of activity in the areas of the brain controlling critical thought. It seems that once we get close to a person, the brain decides the need to assess their character and personality is reduced. The researchers found that both romantic love and maternal love produce the same effect on the brain. They suppress neural activity associated with critical assessment and negative emotions.'

Perhaps this explains why in some cases as romantic love turns to attachment, the level of criticism increases and cracks in once 'perfect' relationships appear. There are, of course, other circumstances where critical reasoning goes into temporary hibernation and the outcome can be shocking ...

ABDICATION OF RESPONSIBILITY

Stanley Milgrim was responsible for one of the most controversial experiments in human psychology. He designed a now infamous test to see if ordinary law-abiding people would give a stranger a lethal electric shock in the name of science. This was to test his theory that destructive obedience was driven by the power of the situation. What percentage of people would obey the experimenter and how many would refuse? The experiment was reenacted in 2009 for a BBC *Horizon* programme, 'How Violent Are You?' The following is a summary of it.

THE EXPERIMENT

Members of the public were invited to be participants in 'a scientific study of memory and learning'. Each participant in turn was introduced to a professor in a white coat, and a fellow volunteer (in fact, both were actors). The professor explains that the test will involve a form of punishment via electric shock. The participant is told that one volunteer will be the teacher and the other the learner. The teacher administers the shocks and the learner receives them. The situation was rigged such that the real participant was always given the role of teacher and the actor was the learner.

The participant is then shown the learner being strapped into an electric chair in one room and electrodes being applied. The teacher is then taken to a separate room with the electric shock generator. This goes from 15v through to 450v (lethal) with a notice saying 'Danger, Extreme Shock XXX'. The participant is given a 45v electric shock so that they know what the punishment feels like. This means the participant is definitely aware that the 'learner' will be experiencing quite high levels of pain.

The professor had no coercive power, and was not able to force anyone to do anything.

The participant (in their teacher role) is provided with a list of word pairs and told that the learner has to memorise them. The teacher then asks the learner a question and if the learner can't answer or gives a wrong answer, the teacher will then administer a shock, with the voltage increasing as time goes on.

After a number of shocks the teacher can hear the learner expressing pain. Subsequently the victim's distress is made clearer and the teacher can hear,

'Let me out, let me out of here. Let me out!'

At this point many of the teachers checked with the professor to see if it was correct to continue. In order to encourage them to do so, participants were told key phrases such as:

● There is no permanent or lasting damage to tissue.
● The experiment requires that you continue.

Milgrim's experiment is designed to find out if the teachers will end the test or obey the professor and administer extremely painful shocks, in the name of science. At voltages of 370v and higher the learner fails to respond, leaving the teacher unclear as to whether they are unconscious or even dead. The participants are told to treat no answer as a wrong answer and continue.

So what percentage of people would obey the professor and go all the way to 450v 'Danger, Extreme Shock XXX'?

RESULTS

A total of 66 per cent of people were prepared to submit the stranger to a lethal 450v shock in the original experiment. Fortunately things have changed since this study was first carried out in 1961. When the experiment was reenacted reassuringly the number of people prepared to kill a stranger had increased to 75 per cent. Now that's what I call progress.

There is still controversy surrounding this experiment and what, exactly, it did test. Milgram said, *'I am certain there is a complex personality basis to obedience and disobedience, but I am certain that I have not found it.'*

Lauren Slater in her book, *Opening Skinner's Box*, discovered some surprising information after interviewing two of the original participants, one who refused to go beyond a certain level, and one who went all the way. The refuser had stopped the experiment not because the person supposedly being given the electric shock was in danger but because they were scared of their own heart failing due to stress! The second participant went through to the end of the experiment but was so affected afterwards by what they had agreed to do that it changed their whole outlook on life. No longer would they blindly bow down and conform to figures of authority.

Was it just obedience to authority that was tested? Perhaps within that is also included 'abdication of responsibility'. Both have some serious implications.

According to recent research neurologists have discovered that the brain sets aside rationality when it gets the benefit of supposedly expert opinion. Financial advice can literally make us take leave of our senses. It is claimed that when an investment adviser makes a recommendation, the brain tends to abdicate responsibility and defer to their authority, with little independent thought.

A team from Emory University, Atlanta found that expert advice suppressed brain activity in a neural circuit known to play a critical role in sound decision making and value judgements. This might be why we are so inclined to follow expert recommendation without questioning it, when a bit of independent thinking might take us down a different route. The researchers reported that people are probably especially susceptible to blindly trusting experts during economic uncertainty.

When people had to make their own decisions, the brain areas responsible for active decision making and calculating probability were very active. When financial advice was given, the very same areas were much less active, suggesting the brain was 'offloading' its work in the presence of an 'expert'.

Professor Gregory Berns, who led the research, said:

> 'This study indicates that the brain relinquishes responsibility when a trusted authority provides expertise. The problem is that it can work to a person's detriment if the trusted source turns out to be incompetent or corrupt.'

This demise of critical reasoning in the face of authority may be shocking, but so too will be the state of your bank balance if you don't protect yourself against the 'experts' in the finance industry.

BAAAAAAAA

Last but not least in the ever-growing set of cognitive tendencies are the social ones, and the one that ranks above all others when it comes to investment is herding/conformity. We may not quite be sheep but it seems we are very partial to a dollop of mint sauce.

In the 1950s Solomon Asch arranged an experiment to test conformity. Participants were divided into groups of six. Asch showed the participants two sets of cards. The first card had a single line of a certain length and the second card had three comparable lines of differing lengths, A, B and C. The participants were asked to select which of the three lines matched the original on the first card (see the following figure).

The correct answer is this case is clearly C, being the same size as the original line. A and B are obviously different lengths (it wasn't an optical illusion test).

The twist was that only one of the group of six was a real subject. This subject was positioned so that they were always second to last to be asked. The experiment started with everyone giving correct answers but then on other rounds the four preceding participants gave false answers to see if the real subject would generally follow the answer the other participants had given. This did not happen every time, but 74 per cent went along with what the group said at least once. In later tests (by, for example, Crutchfield) where more ambiguity was introduced into the possible answers, individuals went with the consensus up to 79 per cent of the time.

When debriefed the actual subjects said they knew the answer they were giving was wrong, but they still followed the group. Conformity may be defined as yielding to group pressure. There are three types of conformity:

1   **Internalisation:** People become persuaded that the group is right; they change their opinion, not just their behaviour.

2 **Compliance:** People believe the group to be wrong but still conform even though they don't change their mind.

3 **Identification:** Everyone else is, so they will too. These people don't think, typical of younger teenagers.

Why do people conform?

● People want to be accepted as part of the group, and don't want to be different.

● People assume that others probably know more than they do, especially if they lack information or do not know the answer.

This 'preference' towards conformity may appear to be more powerful than we think. Eisenberger and Liebermann conducted experiments into social exclusion in 2004. Technology was employed to see which areas of the brain were affected. As reported in *Science* magazine, what they discovered was *'the pain of social exclusion is felt in exactly the same parts of the brain that feel physical pain [and] the brain may treat abstract social experiences and concrete physical experiences as more similar than is generally assumed.'*

So whilst it is more than disturbing to see people cast aside the truth and embrace what they know to be false, as in the Asch experiment, going against the crowd may feel similar to being punched in the face as far as your brain is concerned.

An unholy alliance of wanting to run with the herd, fear in the face of ambiguity and manifestations similar to physical pain appear to be joining forces, all of which will conspire to decrease the quality of our investment decisions.

PROBABILITY VS. UNCERTAINTY

At first glance it would appear that probability and uncertainty are almost identical. However, there is an important difference. In simple terms, probability is measurable and uncertainty isn't. Let's look at an example by returning to the bag of balls.

An opaque cloth bag contains one black ball and one white ball. Given this fact there is a 50 per cent chance of picking a black ball first and a 50 per cent chance of picking a white ball first. Probability (as opposed to uncertainty) has some fixed rules. In this case there are only two balls in the bag, one is black and one is white. Therefore probability applies.

Imagine now that I have left the room to answer the front door to a friend and someone hits a cricket ball through a small gap in the open window and by some miraculous stroke of luck this red ball lands in the bag. Now I return to the bag with my friend (having heard and seen nothing) and declare with 100 per cent certainty (at least in my mind) that he will pick out either a white ball or a black ball from the bag and there is a 50 per cent chance of picking a black ball first. The first ball he picks out is the red cricket ball and my world of probability has just been destroyed because uncertainty has changed the rules of the game. It was never 100 per cent certain that only two balls were in the bag, but it was just incredibly unlikely it would not be the case.

So probability works under a given frame of reference or with limited outcomes or expectations. Uncertainty, on the other hand, does not require a specific set of criteria to be in place for it to occur; this is why in practice many predictive models fail. They do not incorporate the possibility of fraud and highly unlikely events, both of which are eminently possible. Accepting that uncertainty exists will make you better with money.

OUT OF CONTROL

We often think we have more control than we actually have. This is called the illusion of control and a team at Stanford University demonstrated this by splitting students into three groups. The first group was asked to write about a situation where they felt in control. The second group wrote about a time they felt out of control. The third group did no writing. Then students were asked to roll a die, or nominate somebody else to roll for them. They were offered $5 for correctly guessing the number rolled. The 'in control' writing group all opted to roll themselves, compared to just over half of the 'out of control' writing group, and nearly 70 per cent of the control group. This research suggests that the 'in control' group somehow felt they had power over the die and could influence the outcome, despite it being completely random whoever rolled it.

And when it comes to rolling dice, how many of us roll the dice softly when wanting a low number, and throw them hard when we want a high number? That's the illusion of control in operation. Unfortunately, when it comes to investment in, say, the stock market, any control is pretty much illusory.

Resistance is futile?

Self-control is a limited resource. Just like your muscles or energy levels it tires with use or, as James Montier puts it, 'each effort at self-control reduces the amount available for subsequent self-control efforts.'

EXAMPLE

In self-control research, people were asked to resist temptation by eating radishes instead of the cookies and chocolate on display alongside. The group that did so gave up on a subsequent frustrating task more quickly than participants who hadn't been asked to use their self-control. This and similar studies concluded that those asked to exert self-control had depleted some kind of mental resource meaning they had less in reserve to call on in a second task.

So not only do we have a high propensity for taking immediate pleasures over delayed rewards, but the more we resist the harder it becomes to do so.

RISK IT, FOR A BISCUIT

Let's be honest. Humans are bad at assessing risk and probability. We get ourselves into a lather over issues that are highly improbable and at the same time we ignore the ones we should be more worried about. Why? More biases, of course.

Availability bias

Definition: The easier it is to recall examples, the more common or likely that thing is judged to be. A tendency to overestimate probabilities of events associated with memorable or vivid occurrences.

> **EXAMPLE**
>
> You are much more likely to die in a car accident than a plane accident, and your child is more likely to die in an accident than be abducted. But the majority thinks the inverse, because the less likely events are more available (more memorable). Negative images are recalled more easily.

Recency bias

Definition: Attaching higher importance or weighting to more recent events/observations.

NB: This is different to availability bias as it refers to the most recent information as opposed to the most vivid, or easiest to recall. However, given that we tend to cull memories there is often a significant crossover between the two.

But it's not even as simple as just these: we are also governed by what Dan Gardner, in his book, *Risk*, refers to as **the good/ bad rule** and this seems to be more bad than good. Originally called 'the affect heuristic', Paul Slovac demonstrated using students (the guinea pig of choice to the intelligentsia, it seems) that if people thought the risks posed by something were high, they judged the benefits to be low and vice versa, if they thought the benefit was high, the risk was seen as low. Risk and benefit were inversely correlated.

So take sunbathing, for example: lying on a beach in the Caribbean sounds (and feels) good so the risk from radiation exposure is deemed low, even if it isn't. Our instinct initially shouts 'good' or 'bad' and then the judgement that follows is heavily influenced by that initial call. As Gardner puts it: '*Is this thing likely to kill me? It feels good. Good things don't kill. So, no, don't worry about it.*'

Here we are, back with System 1, the 'Speedy Gonzales' of the neural world, able to render a judgement in an instant, but this brilliant system is also flawed, relying on rules of thumb that generate irrational conclusions.

Maybe we need to spend a little time improving our risk literacy. Given that the internet has allowed access to almost unlimited data sources it is important that people understand and interpret the available data. Risk literacy is also critical in being able to make sensible life choices, especially on health and money.

Professor David Spiegelhalter, at the University of Cambridge, is keen to address this point and has set up a roadshow that travels around schools to teach kids about risk. He uses examples that at first glance appear to be strange but when you look at the statistics, are not. For example, the case of a Gloucestershire family where despite the three children being of different ages, all three siblings were born on exactly the same calendar date.

The chances of this happening are approximately 1 in 135,000. Given there are one million families in the UK with three children, then one would expect not only one family where this occurred but seven. Given the correct sample size, the incredibly freaky becomes the highly probable.

Professor Spiegelhalter: *'It's very difficult to think calmly about uncertainty. That's why it needs to be taught.'* I certainly don't recall being taught much about uncertainty at school. We learned a bit about probability, i.e. there was about a one in ten chance you would get caught when smoking behind the bike sheds.

When interviewed by Mark Henderson in *The Times*, Spiegelhalter gave several rules of risk but without doubt the most notable is his observation with respect to predictions:

66 *We cannot predict exactly how every precise event will turn out, but we can often predict the overall pattern of events surprisingly well.* 99

Where we definitely struggle with understanding risk is with low probability/high consequence events such as the Asian Tsunami. Experts had warned in advance that it would happen, they just didn't know when. The cost of an early warning system was minimal but no one listened: 230,000 people lost their lives because of that error of judgement. It's the same with earthquakes. People buy earthquake insurance immediately after an earthquake when the risk of occurrence may be low but do not do so even when the risks are highest and they are warned one is coming. This is the availability heuristic taking full effect – if you have to struggle to remember one, there is nothing to worry about, is there? Who personally remembers the 1929 Crash?

One definition of risk is:

$$risk = probability \times consequence$$

Small probabilities add up when chances are repeatedly taken, as any long-term Russian roulette player will tell you, providing you can find one that isn't pushing up daisies.

We live in a society that does not understand risk. We are becoming increasingly risk-averse, burdened by absurd legislation and precautions to remove risk. Perhaps more understanding and less legislation is the way forward. Or, given all the biases we have come across in this chapter, should we just give up and resign ourselves to failure? Not necessarily. As Ellen Peters discovered, people who are more numerate are less likely to be misdirected by their natural instincts.* We can intervene and correct ourselves if we put our minds to it, and because not everyone will do so, therein lies an opportunity.

PREDICTABLE AND IRRATIONAL?

'People make mistakes when they invest ... but they do so in a predictable fashion.' We have seen in this chapter that being irrational may have benefits in certain circumstances but in the context of investment it appears many of those traits could be bad news. However, as Dan Ariely points out, we are 'predictably irrational' and given that there is a predictability in people's irrational behaviour this may offer a number of opportunities for those willing to embrace and challenge the forces that shape our decisions.

Humans are contradictory creatures when it comes to risk and fear. As James Montier eloquently puts it: 'Without emotion we can't sense risk but with emotion we can't control the fear that risk generates.' Perhaps we should return to Damasio for the final word: 'What makes you and me "rational" is not suppressing our emotions, but tempering them in a positive

---

* Probability lessons may teach children how to weigh life's odds and be winners.

way.' And this is the proposed objective for anybody wanting to become 'the smart money'.

Now that we have a little better understanding of our foibles, what does this mean in practice? What are the implications and can we improve our monetary decisions? We'll return to all these points and what to do about them in Chapter 7, but one way to improve our decision making is by learning to ignore everyone.

CHAPTER 4

Ignore everyone

Stop the press and join the noise abatement society

Believe nothing, no matter where you read it or who has said it, not even if I have said it, unless it agrees with your own reason and your own common sense BUDDHA

People only ever lie for two reasons; either because they are ashamed of the truth; or because they don't think you are fit to know the truth – or both TERENCE FRISBY

PORKY PIES

On Saturday 4 October 2008 Mr Sismey-Durrant, chief executive of Icesave, was interviewed on BBC Radio 4. When asked if UK Icesave customers could be sure their money was safe and they could get it out of the bank, he answered: '*Yes, they can be*' and added '*they shouldn't be nervous about the state of the bank.*' Three days later the bank was bust.

Even those who wanted to get at their money couldn't, because the website wasn't working, but this was described by Sismey-Durrant as, 'A glitch, not a failure'. Worse, some customers had their withdrawal transactions on Friday 3 October reversed on Tuesday 7 October, five days after the withdrawal date. Jump forward three years to 2011 and what do you know, it turns out Landsbanki (parent company of Icesave) illegally transferred millions of pounds of British savers' money ... So, that's bank CEOs off the list of who to listen to.

Our expectations are that people in positions of responsibility and power are going to tell the truth. And while many are fairly honest, many are not, and this is unlikely to ever change. But dishonesty is only one of the reasons to be wary of what people tell us. We still have to add in manipulation, manufacturing consent, vested interest, cover-ups, laziness, incompetence, and that's before we get started on all the crap predictions, and cognitive biases we met in Chapter 3. If you genuinely believe that what you read in the mainstream media is balanced, unbiased commentary and reporting, please stop reading now. Just book yourself a one-way trip to la-la land and suck on the 22ft dandelion and burdock lollipop waiting for you in the arrivals hall. For everyone else it's a trip back to the circus and a CSI investigation into why so many 'dead bodies' are lying around.

WHY 97 PER CENT ARE WRONG

For those readers that skipped over the Introduction to this book, shame on you. As a doff to the shameful, the inattentive and erstwhile sufferers from short-term memory loss, the analogy of the circus knife thrower was given:

> 'Imagine you are a circus knife thrower who gets it wrong 97 per cent of the time. Chances are that your career might be almost as short-lived as your assistants.'

The 97 per cent failure rate was not a statistic pulled out of thin air but an accuracy level of economists in predicting contractions (economic, not maternal).

> 'A recent study looked at "consensus forecasts" (the predictions of large groups of economists) that were made in advance of 60 different national recessions that hit around the world in the '90s: *in 97 percent of the cases*, the study found, the economists failed to predict the coming contraction a year in advance ... worse, many of the economists failed to anticipate recessions that occurred as soon as two months later.'
>
> Stephen Mihm, *The New York Times*

Even by today's rickety exam grade devaluation standards this seems an astonishingly weak strike ratio. So if our professional knife thrower had the same hit rate as a professional economist there would be 97 dead assistants in every 100 employed! Is it even worth getting out of bed and going to work with this level of inaccuracy? Economics is not called the dismal science because it is dull, it's because it's not very scientific. Put another way, it's not as simple as an apple falling on your head and calling it gravity. Most economists are human (optimists) and the mathematical models employed are also optimistic and based on probability not uncertainty, or put another way – wrong.

On top of this malingering inaccuracy you have the different schools of thought, e.g. classical, neo-classical, socialist, Chicago (monetarism), Austrian (no compromise) and that's before we get to the contemporary offshoots like behavioural finance. And like a set of cantankerous old people mouthing off at each other in a nursing home they never seem to agree on very much at all. Or as the First Law of Economics states, *'for every economist there exists an equal and opposite economist.'*

Now if you'd like to see a proper scrap it doesn't get any better than *Fight of the Century: Keynes vs Hayek, Part II* directed by John Papola on YouTube. Probably the most enjoyable nine minutes of economics in existence.

Perhaps the various schools should have listened to President Lyndon Johnson when he remarked, *'Making a speech on economics ... is a lot like pissing down your leg. It seems hot to you, but it never does to anyone else.'*

If the economists can't agree on what's going on or more importantly what to do about it, maybe we should just ignore them as well.

JAW ON THE FLOOR

Someone we should definitely be ignoring is a prize-winning journalist; we'll come to the non-prize winners in the next section. While there were some pretty incredible journalistic faux-pas during the 2008 financial crisis, king of the hill has to go to Anatole Kaletsky, or as his marketing micro-biography said at the time, *'one of the leading commentators on economics ... who has won many awards for his financial and political journalism.'* Unfortunately there is not enough space to highlight everyone's errors so let's just take an excerpt from this high-profile writer of *The Times*.

This book has no personal axe to grind with Mr Kaletsky (or any other individual reporters), after all, he appears to be an intelligent and insightful writer. However, there is one major flaw – during the financial crisis Part I, he was wrong by a country mile. Let's remind ourselves of some of his headlines, observations and analyses.

25 FEBRUARY 2008

HEADLINE: BEAR MARKET: THIS IS THE LATEST BUYING OPPORTUNITY

NB: Between February and November 2008 the FTSE crashed by 33 per cent.

7 APRIL 2008

'I am probably the only economist left in the world who still believes that a US recession is likely to be avoided.'

Readjusted statistics later showed the US had entered a recession at the end of 2007.

5 MAY 2008

HEADLINE: CREDIT CRUNCH FAILS TO PRODUCE FEARED ECONOMIC CATASTROPHE

'So the sky did not fall in. While the Chicken Littles of the world economy … may still repeat mechanically the IMF's surprising judgment that the world – especially America – faces its worst financial crisis since the 1930s.'

Chicken Little is now a prophet, apparently.

16 JUNE 2008

'Why does anyone still think that the US economy is in recession?' 'So let me stick my neck out and say without qualification – the US economy is out of the woods.'

It wasn't.

28 JULY 2008

'A theme of this column for almost a year has been the contrast between apocalyptic views in the financial markets about the earth-shattering consequences of the credit crunch and the rather more mundane evidence from the real economy of a mild recession, at worst.'

'Mr Gross maintained that no end was in sight for the housing slump: US housing, he insisted, is the world's "one asset class that all observers can agree is going down". Except that it isn't.'

2008 was the worst housing slump in the US since the Great Depression.

20 SEPT 2008
HEADLINE: AFTER A BREATHLESS WEEK, I'M OPTIMISTIC AGAIN

'So the impossible has become inevitable – and even faster than I expected.'

'The violent zig-zags of the past two weeks … have left everyone dizzy. Not least readers of these pages, many of whom have complained about the way I lurched from optimism to pessimism in analysing the past few weeks' events.'

One has at least to admire the consistency of Mr Kaletsky's stance in the face of overwhelming evidence to the contrary.

So, after over a year of self-confessed denial, followed by a brief wobble, everything was suddenly optimistic again on 20 September. Of course, this was just before the main panic in October and November 2008. The point is, how many people are sucked up into these hospital passes and base their investment decisions on 'the worst is over before it's even begun' or 'it's not actually happening'? This is market noise of the highest order. Ignore prize winners.

SPONGE ME DOWN

While Mr Kaletsky was being a member of the *'confederacy of dunces'* (his words, not mine) at least he understands the technical aspects of finance and financial journalism. Imagine what happens when the new kid on the financial journalistic block gets sent to cover the City. Like SpongeBob Squarepants, but without the pants, it involves soaking up a hell of a lot of old tosh spewed from the banks' PR departments and then regurgitating it to the general public. Of course, the reporters aren't that stupid. They may not know the difference between a merger and an acquisition but before publicly spouting whatever company line the banks choose to feed them they make sure they get taken to a premium sporting occasion on the banks' expenses. It's a case of 'you scratch my back and I'll give you a full aromatherapy body massage and a happy ending.'*

One former head of PR at a leading bank (both shall remain nameless to protect the guilty) highlighted these three points:

- Relationships between PR executives and journalists can be very strong, often crossing over into genuine friendships – through lunches, corporate hospitality etc. Many PR executives are ex-journalists themselves. As a result they can bring a great deal of influence to bear, often minimising the impact of a story. They can steer journalists in another direction or play down the size of story or, in some cases, offer something else up in return for a story not being written, i.e. there's lots of room for negotiation/subtle manipulation.

- Journalists rely very heavily on their sources, i.e. bankers/ PR executives, and do not want to burn bridges.

*The UK Bribery Act that came into force in 2011 may mean the ending isn't as pleasurable as it once was.

Newsrooms are also fairly understaffed so there isn't time
for much investigative reporting. As a result journalists will
often take press releases at face value and accept a story
planted with them by the PR dept.

● The media can have a herd mentality so sometimes smaller
stories can be blown out of all proportion as journalists
can pick up on what has been written in one of the early
reports (particularly if on the wires or if following up on
news broken in a daily paper). If the initial coverage hypes
something up – or even misses the main point – there's a
chance that will continue throughout any ensuing coverage.

Result: ignore junior journos as well as prize-winning ones.

MANUFACTURING CONSENT

Having shown that bank managers, economists, journalists
and other individuals are more than capable of feeding you
large dollops of misleading information it is time to look at
the mass media as a corporate entity. Incisive dissection of the
news media and how it really works has been well documented
by Noam Chomsky. Many of the news media outlets are run
by large corporations and are therefore subject to commercial
and competitive pressures as well as the whims of the elites that
control them. Chomsky presents the media as a propaganda
model where news is distorted not only by what items are
selected to report on but in the manner, angle and emphasis of
delivery. Whilst some of it is deliberate and conscious, there is
also much unconscious and unintentional bias.

So, in addition to Prof. Spiegelhalter's recommendations we
met in Chapter 3 on understanding risk, you might want to add
in some anti-manipulation lessons to help decipher commercial or
political messages. Although the only educational establishment of
which I am aware that offers it specifically in their curriculum is
The Humanitarian School in Moscow, founded by Vasiliy Bogin.

Whatever else you do, learn to automatically question the quality of information that is presented to you on a daily basis. It is very easy to forget when reading an individual article or opinion that what is being stated could be utter bunkum. It is therefore essential that you choose your sources of information wisely.

Of course the media play an essential role in uncovering everything from misdemeanours to outrageous frauds and so, as with life, it's all shades of grey. For more black and white examples of whom you should be ignoring then look for those with a vested interest.

VESTED INTEREST

Don't walk into a barber's shop and ask if you need a haircut, or ask a lawyer if you have a good case prior to engaging them. Both can perform a Sweeney Todd, it's just a question of which one will do the heaviest scalping (it's the lawyer, in case you were confused – Todd only went for a partial decapitation).

Don't ever expect impartial advice from people who are going to earn money from you signing on the dotted line. First questions should always be 'Who is telling me the information?' and 'What do they have to gain?' If the answer involves your 'hard earned' then tread carefully.

As we will see in more detail later, this is why you will never hear a fund manager from the financial services industry telling you to sell your shares. Quite simply, if you remove your money from the markets you are reducing someone's wages. Therefore no one in the industry is ever going to publicly tell you to get out of the market. It's the exception that proves the rule and Hugh Hendry became one of the few fund managers to tell it like it really is in a round table discussion published in *The Sunday Times*:

> 'Come on, guys, wake up! The problem is everyone here has to sell financial products and as soon as you say you are

pessimistic, or bearish, or God forbid you say sell, someone
from the hierarchy comes down and tells you to shut up.'

As soon as you understand this point then it pulls everyone's motives into perspective. Returning to Icesave and Mr
Sismey-Durrant's comments, which bank manager is ever
going to tell you their bank is vulnerable when, as we saw
in Chapter 1, banking is a confidence trick? Admitting the
truth would ensure the collapse. The only thing Sismey-
Durrant could have saved is his reputation and unfortunately
nowadays few people seem to value theirs as highly as they
should.

What we need are people with a fierce independent streak
but please don't get confused. There has so far been little
independence to independent financial advisors (IFAs). The sad
truth is that far too many 'independent' financial advisors were
more interested in what made them money, not what would
make your money grow. In the past most IFAs have sold the
product that brings them the fattest returns through hidden/
trailing commissions. Thankfully this has now been addressed
and is a topic we will return to in Chapter 7.

What about real estate? House prices going down? No one
in the business will say so. At least not until well after the event
and it's getting too embarrassing to still be in denial, although
this can take years.

Grant Bovey, property developer and husband of TV
presenter Anthea Turner, resorted to the classic Robert Maxwell
defence tactic to convince everyone there wasn't a problem with
his property business: 'I will sue anyone who says that Imagine
Homes is in financial difficulty.'

It went bust shortly afterwards but not before he could issue
one of the most quotable business lines ever delivered:

> “ *We have huge profits that have*
> *yet to materialise.* ”

So strike most fund managers, independent financial advisors and real estate developers/agents off the list of who to listen to. Anyone else?

ANALYSE THIS

Analysts are specialists who are meant to be able to offer some insight into a company's share price and indicate whether it offers fair value. Recommendations to buy, hold or sell are made after analysing a company 'in depth'. A very useful source, or at least it would be if it were in any way accurate. Analysts suffer from rampant optimism, vested interest and regularly overestimate earnings.

More worryingly there is an innate desire to encourage people to trade so that more transactional commissions can be generated. However, enunciating the word *sell* seems to be more linguistically challenging than the word *buy*. The years 2007 to 2008 saw one of the worst downturns in stock market history. Under such circumstances one would surely expect to see an increase in 'sell' recommendations? Err, no!

Look at the chart overleaf. While buy recommendations diminished and hold recommendations increased, the number of sells stayed consistently flat. Urban linguistics lesson number 1: Hold = Sell.

We know that making predictions is notoriously difficult so often analysts' calls will end up clustering together. On average analysts, like 'sound bankers', would rather be wrong together than go out on a limb by making estimates that later prove to be conspicuously inaccurate.

In the indomitable words of Naseem Taleb, '*Stock market analysts have proved to be worse than nothing.*' Recommendation: ignore analysts.

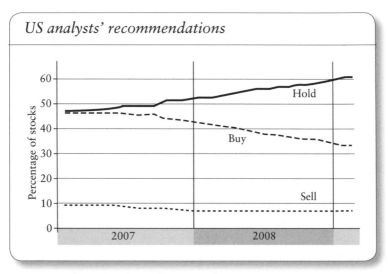

Source: Data from Bloomberg/*The New York Times*

ILLUSION OF KNOWLEDGE

Analysts and many others within the financial services industry have an information and data obsession. The inference being that more information leads to better decision making. This is the illusion of knowledge. In fact more information beyond a basic level doesn't improve the quality of decision making but does lead to overconfidence and information overload. The important gets mixed up with the irrelevant. In one experiment (Handzic), participants were asked to estimate ice-cream sales on Bondi beach using three equally weighted critical factors, namely ambient air temperature, hours of sunshine and number of visitors. The results from the group with less information outperformed those with more. Conclusion: It is best to concentrate on a few key variables and ignore the information deluge.

Frank Skinner, the English comedian experienced what can go horribly wrong when the illusion of knowledge is offered by others. Frank put all his money into Coutts, the Queen's bankers, on the assumption that it would therefore be safe. It might have been if he hadn't been advised to put it all into AIG, the American Insurance Group that was subsequently bailed out in 2008. When he queried that fact that all the money was in one basket he was informed the worst case scenario would be a ten per cent loss but there was no way that could actually happen. After the worst did happen, and some more on top, Skinner was then told he would have to wait four years to find out whether he could have the other half of his millions back. It was George Carman QC who in court famously quipped, *'Some accountants are comedians, but comedians are never accountants.'* Perhaps we now have a new twist on that gem *'Some bankers are comedians, but comedians are never bankers.'* In this case, it's the comedian who better understood the risk, he just fell foul of the brain's diminishment of critical reasoning in the face of 'expert' advice as we saw in Chapter 3. Here is some free advice – ignore 'experts'.

SEVEN DEADLY SINS

This concept was formulated by James Montier after realising that fund managers, despite their training and market knowledge, suffer from the same cognitive biases as everyone else.

Gluttony (information gluttony)

Too much information and the illusion of knowledge have been covered in the previous section but what of the others?

Lust (company love-ins)

Fund managers meeting with company executives search out information that will confirm their own perceptions (confirmation bias) rather than take a more sceptical approach. It is also difficult to tell whether executives are being economical with the truth and therefore meetings are likely to be just as detrimental as they are helpful. Or put another way – a waste of time.

Wrath (group-based decisions)

Conformity and herding is prevalent in meetings. It is often difficult to propose counter-arguments to the group view without the risk of being ostracised. It's the Solomon Asch experiment that we saw in Chapter 3 revisited in real life. Those differing markedly from the leaders view may endure a mild dose of wrath at some stage in the proceedings. Group decisions tend to amplify rather than alleviate the biases within the decision-making process and are very bad at uncovering hidden information.

Sloth (believing everything you read)

Humans are suckers for a story. *'In theory we gather evidence, weigh it up and then decide, in reality we gather evidence* [badly and with bias], *create a story based on it and then match the story to a decision.'* This tends to drive investors into areas that they would otherwise avoid.

The size of impact a story can make is demonstrated by an experiment involving a mock trial:

> 'When the prosecution presented the evidence in a story order, but the defence presented evidence in witness order, 78% of jurors found the suspect guilty. However, when the formats were reversed only 31% of jurors found the suspect guilty!'
>
> J. Montier, *Behavioural Investing*

And don't forget, modern day official statistics are generally a manipulated government fantasy.

Avarice (short time horizons for investment)

Driven by greed and the need to meet short-term performance targets, fund managers, like other investors, are looking like they are suffering Attention Deficit Hyperactivity Disorder (ADHD). Speculation is usurping investment mentality.

Envy (outsmarting the competition)

Everyone thinks they can outsmart everyone else. The market is characterised by one and two steps of strategic thinking. It has been shown that most fund managers can't beat the market and certainly not consistently. There is now the suggestion that some fund managers are resorting to 'closet trackers' (a tracker being a low-cost option for automatically following the market) rather than being beaten by their compatriots. Peer envy is alive and well and not just in the male toilets.

Pride (forecasting)

Investors are hopeless at forecasting but many fund managers use this as the foundation stone of their strategy and are proud of it. Overoptimism and overconfidence tarnishes this process further; *'The worst performers are generally the most overconfident ... such individuals suffer a double curse of being unskilled and unaware of it.'* Montier also found that just like the overconfident drivers at Princeton University (Chapter 3), 75 per cent of fund managers think they are above average at their jobs.

As we saw with Coutts, the experts are not as expert as they think.

EXCEPTIONS TO THE RULE

The title to this fourth chapter is, of course, a little tongue-in-cheek. It would be unwise to ignore absolutely everyone but it is clear that many of the sources that people rely on are the wrong ones. Hopefully you can see, after reading this chapter, that you are constantly bombarded by utter rubbish. And the precarious towers of tosh coming out of the financial markets can be even worse – and that's before we get to the plain confusing:

66 *When I read the 120 contradictory bits of advice in the* **FT** *alone, I find myself asking the question: who is an expert?* 99 **Jeremy Grantham, GMO**

If you are now somewhat disillusioned after being told who not to listen to, you will be pleased to know that a few pointers in the right direction will be given in Chapter 7.

It's time to wake up and smell the coffee. If you behave like the mindless majority you are unlikely to be successful. The next chapters will show you why the majority are nearly always wrong when it comes to markets, but how does one sort the wheat from the disinformation and chaff? Perhaps we should be asking a tall dark stranger?

CHAPTER 5

Rub my crystal ball

The dismal science partially demystified

History never repeats itself but sometimes it rhymes MARK TWAIN

The farther back you look, the farther you are likely to see WINSTON CHURCHILL

RHYME ON TIME

The quote from Mark Twain on the previous page offers arguably the eight most important words with respect to investing. In fact, Anthony Bolton says that it should be 'burned into the desk of every fund manager'. Why? Because whilst we can never predict the future with absolute *certainty*, the future can be anticipated with a much higher *likelihood* if we can find the correct repetitive pattern or 'rhyme' to follow. Most economic models don't work because they fail to build in uncertainty; scenarios as opposed to models are a more sensible way forward and here history can help.

Understand the bigger picture or get the right narrative and investment decisions become quicker, easier and more profitable. Any knowledge that can swing the financial odds in your favour has to be of interest, doesn't it? Repetitive historical cycles of economic activity and human behaviour exist and are worth knowing about.

Let's begin by looking at two different but essential patterns. Understanding these will allow other pieces to fall into place. Let's start with a cycle that is dear to every Englishman's heart, his (or her) castle.

THREE HOUSE RULES

Most people will have four big investments in their lifetime: themselves, their family, property and a retirement income generator, e.g. savings and/or a pension. Whilst the initial two are undoubtedly the most important, the latter two will be our focus from here on in. Little time will be devoted to the UK property market, not because it is superfluous or less important (for many readers their biggest investment will be in property), but because investing in it successfully can all be summed up in three simple rules. Here we have the perfect example of Occam's razor being applied to a complex situation and producing a very clear and simple approach that works. Armed with this knowledge people who know nothing about investing in property can outwit many of the so-called experts. Moreover it demonstrates the power of repetitive patterns. So what is the little known secret of the UK property market?

House Rule Number 1:
The UK property market has thus far
followed an 18-year cycle.*

Fred Harrison has studied the UK property market going all the way back to 1800. He discovered a cyclical pattern that has repeated approximately every 18 years – 14 years of boom followed by four years of bust. According to Phil Anderson, author of *The Secret Life of Real Estate,* this approximate pattern has also applied in the US for the last 200 years. In fact, Anderson points out this 14-year cycle of rising prices, followed by four years of declining prices has been happening in most Western economies where land is privately owned since at least 1955. So what's occurring?

House Rule Number 2:
Location, Location, Location.

This concept should already be familiar to everyone. A ten-bedroom house, for example in prime location central London, is worth millions. Put it in downtown Detroit and its worth considerably less. Quite simply, location matters. But there is one component of house prices that matters more than the rest – the price of the land.

*World wars tend to disrupt it.

As Anderson puts it:

> 'A house costs pretty much the same to build, wherever you
> build it – wages are the same, and materials costs are the same.
> But the selling price will depend on the location. That money
> doesn't go to the workers building the house, nor is it spent on
> improving the materials used. It purely benefits the owner of
> the land.'

The figure below shows how disproportionate the land
component of property prices in the UK had become between
1983 and 2007.

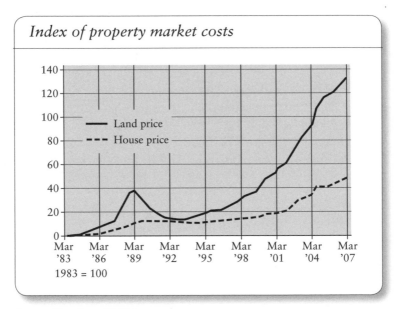

Source: Data from TEAM research

Harrison links land prices directly to the economic cycle:

> 'The supply of land is fixed, so when the economy is growing,
> it has to become more expensive. Rising land prices squeeze
> corporate profits, reducing the money available for wages,

until prices simply can't go any higher because most people can no longer afford to buy.'

In fact, Harrison goes one step further than just linking land and house prices to the economic cycle, he proposes that it actually drives it and this is why the 'experts' get it so wrong.

> 66 *My research suggests that property is the key factor that shapes the business cycle, not the other way around.* 99

Whilst the concept of locational value, or economic rent, is not new (it was first proposed by an English economist called David Ricardo), it has allowed Fred Harrison to make some accurate predictions. The prediction of a fall in 2008 was made by him in November 2005, so the downturn was not a hindsight call. In fact, he called the last one in 1989 as well. Of course the usual disclaimers apply; 'Past performance does not necessarily reflect the future', but as a general rule of thumb the discovery of this pattern has to serve at least as a good starting point.

Cycles are clearly not 100 per cent bulletproof but house prices are far from just being random. Knowledge is power as they say, that's why we have an education system. It's just a shame it doesn't teach you this. Still after that mansion? Good. There is one more hurdle to negotiate:

House Rule Number 3:
House prices are a function of the credit available.

One of the biggest myths peddled prior to 2008 was: 'There is a shortage of housing in the UK.' High demand coupled with a lack of supply always leads to higher prices, right? Well it may have appeared that way for a number of years but the myth was actually a truth missing an adjective. It should have read:

'There is a shortage of *affordable* housing in the UK.' What's the difference?

Kevin and Tracy live on a minimum wage and need some extra space. Kevin wants to buy Buckingham Palace but is about £200 million short of his target. Kevin's neighbours also suffer from delusions of grandeur and also want to buy Buckingham Palace but are in a similar predicament to Kevin. Result, there is a high *perceived* demand for Buckingham Palace but only a small *actual* demand. To increase actual demand Kevin or his pals must each obtain a loan of £200 million (and persuade Queen Liz to sell up). If Liz has numerous offers of £200 million for her main residence one might guess the price is going to increase (this is actual supply and demand). Finally, Kevin and Tracy have to want to take on the £200 million debt in the first instance. Hence House Rule Number 3, house prices are a function of the credit available *combined with people's willingness* to take on that level of debt. If *aspiration* were the only required factor, most of the world would be living in palaces, gin or otherwise.

The amount of credit offered as a mortgage loan depends on several factors, prevailing interest rates and the ability of the applicant to repay the loan being the main ones. Low interest rates equate to lower interest repayments leading to increased affordability. More affordability leads to bigger loans as people like to live in larger houses (as opposed to the undersized breeder boxes currently under construction). Bank lending standards ease if house prices go up as they are backed by an increasing asset. So where is the problem?

As with land prices, credit moves in cycles too. If land prices drive the housing market, as James Ferguson remarked, 'Credit is the fuel in the engine.' Credit in general had been loosening in the UK since the 1970s and particularly from the 1990s to 2007. From a brief peak in UK interest rates at 15 per cent they tumbled to 5 per cent and then went much lower. As credit availability expands, prices tend to go up, when it decreases prices generally go down. Humans tend to have short-term memories.

After 15 years of living in a benign economic environment, people forgot that credit availability could be reversed. Now everyone knows it. Welcome to the credit crunch.

So just when you think you have completely understood the system along comes government intervention and low interest rates to artificially manipulate the market. Keeping interest rates low means, in theory, the housing market should not fall as quickly as it otherwise would have 'normally'. Mortgage repayments are lower and therefore more affordable.

The problem is that whilst the government and central bank control interest rates most of the time, if you have a massive debt mountain (as we do) there are others who occasionally get a say in the matter – the people who buy our debt.

Our national debt exists in the form of bonds. A bond is simply a long-term loan. Anyone who buys one of these bonds receives interest on the money they have loaned to the government. At the end of the term the original amount of the loan is paid back.*

The fly in the ointment for the government and the central bank (and therefore you, the taxpayer) is that in the end it may not be 'we' who decide what the rates will be, it's the people buying our enormous debt mountain who occasionally get the last laugh. Or as Blofeld once remarked whilst stroking his snow-white merkin, '*We meet again, Mr Bond.*' It was James Carville who said, '*I used to think if there was reincarnation …*
I want to come back as the bond market. You can intimidate everyone.'

The bond market (the total number of entities that partake in buying bonds) is where the real power is; if it loses confidence in a country's ability to pay its sovereign debt then it asks for a higher rate of return to offset the risk and up go the interest rates. At which point your large mortgage repayments may remind you of that certain quote, '*Bend over, Blackadder, it's*

---

* Usually.

poker time' – but without the associated jocularity because it's actually you that's on the receiving end.

This is why other metrics are a better measure of long-term value than the plat du jour 'affordability'. Affordability depends on whether you still have a job, the bank still wants you as a customer and the interest rate level. It is sometimes said that people buy a repayment level, not a house price, but rates vary and just because they hit a 300-year low in the UK there is no guarantee they will stay there.

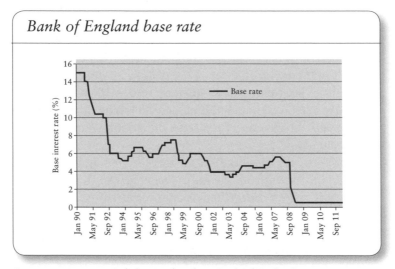

Bank of England base rate

Source: www.economicshelp.org; data from Bank of England

We will return to what metrics really matter when it comes to valuations in the final chapter, but before leaving the housing market and looking at other patterns there is one more general but vital point to address and that is the issue of price vs value.

HOW MUCH?

Let's return to the land that time forgot (Chapter 1) and recall the woolly mammoths example. Cavemen Ted wanted a new spear so he went to see Ugg. 'That'll be two woolly mammoths, please,' said Ugg – until there was a shortage of mammoths and the price suddenly increased. The example was crude but hopefully effective in explaining how the value of 'money', in this case woolly mammoth meat, changed over time depending on circumstances. Money should be a store of value but paper money, i.e. currencies, often aren't, especially when politicians find themselves in a hole and the printing presses get rolling. This should make you think seriously about what unit you should be measuring in. We have all been indoctrinated into believing we can only measure the financial value of an item using paper money. But if the value of that money is constantly changing, is this wise?

Imagine trying to build a table and the ruler you were using changed length every time you measured? A good friend recently employed a carpenter who, judging by the finished results, may have had access to one of these magical sticks. Any sensible 'chippy' would, however, under those circumstances, select an alternative measurement method. When it comes to financial measurement, perhaps so should you?

> 66 *Money is not wealth but the yardstick by which modern cultures measure wealth.* 99 **J. Greer**

Paper money is so ubiquitous that we perhaps forget it's only there as a medium to pay for goods that are actually useful. Food, shelter, warmth, services and all the other nonsense on top of our basic needs are what we expect to get with it. For example, the GBP doesn't look like a great store of value if you look at the figure on page 104.

The pound kept its value for over 150 years and then, from 1900, it didn't. In short, what you can buy with £1 has declined considerably over the past 100 years. The pound was a store of value as well as a medium of exchange. It is no longer the former, only the latter and if you think paper money is a good place to put your savings in the current environment you are sadly mistaken. How mistaken we will see later on.

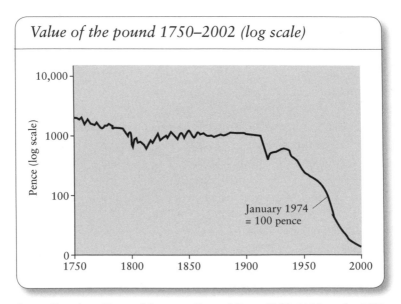

Source: Data from House of Commons Research Paper 03/82, 11 November 2003

For now you should note that while the **price** of something can be rising in pound terms, the **value** of it can be falling. This seems counterintuitive but is true – think back to the Zimbabwean 100 trillion dollar banknote. Value being what it can actually buy in real terms or what it can be exchanged for at any particular moment. Look at the graphs opposite.

It doesn't have to be gold we measure in; it could be oil, rice or water or anything else. So paper money has its uses as a convenient medium of exchange but it also has its limitations and shortcomings because it can be easily manipulated and hasn't maintained its buying power against 'real' items.

So we have seen that cyclical patterns exist and can often be used to help simplify complex situations. Are there any patterns that could have indicated what was to happen with the financial system? If you follow Generational Dynamics the pattern springs out like a jack-in-the-box handcuffed to a cruise missile.

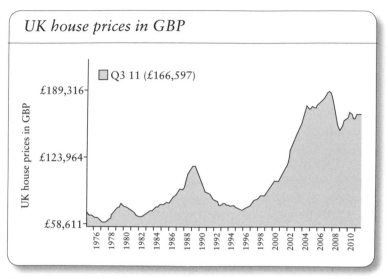

UK house prices in GBP

□ Q3 11 (£166,597)

Source: www.nationwide.co.uk

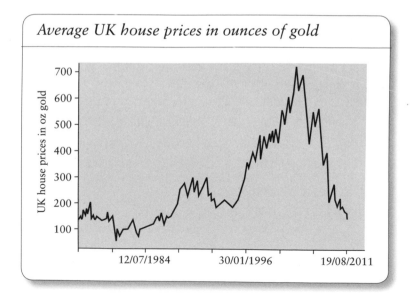

Average UK house prices in ounces of gold

GENERATIONAL DYNAMICS

Not the most inspiring name in the world it has to be said, but it is a fascinating idea. The name is descriptive so let's stick with it. In simple terms the theory states that there is a pattern that repeats itself approximately every 70 to 80 years based on the changing of human generations. This is best summed up by John J. Xenakis on his Generational Dynamics (GD) website:

> 'Generational Dynamics is based on a simple idea: That societies and nations make mistakes and then learn lessons from those mistakes. But generations grow older, retire and die, and are replaced by new generations who are too young to remember those mistakes and those lessons. When that happens? The mistakes are repeated.'

The generations are naturally split into four groups, each covering 20 years, making an 80-year period. These generational groups are given names and allocated typical characteristics. We will only concern ourselves with the full cycle and its supposed impact on the financial world.

Financial crises are nothing new. As we know from Chapters 1 and 2, the financial system is inherently unstable, and therefore we will continue to enjoy crises from time to time. In fact, there have been hundreds of them (over 250 according to Rogoff and Reinhart) but Generational Dynamics argues that prior to 2007 there had been five major international financial crises in the last 400 years:

1   1637 Tulip mania.

2   1720 South Sea Bubble.

3   1789 Bankruptcy of the French monarchy.

4   1857 Panic of.

5   1929 Wall Street Crash.

These are termed 'generational crashes' because they occur roughly every 70 to 80 years. Xenakis explains:

> 'Just as the generation of people who lived through the last one have all disappeared, the younger generations have resumed the same dangerous credit securitisation practices that led to the previous generational crash. After each of these generational crashes, the survivors impose new rules or laws to make sure that it never happens again. As soon as those survivors are dead, the new generations ignore the rules, thinking that they're just for "old people", and a new generational crash occurs.'

This type of pattern was supported by Nikolai Kondratiev, although his timescales were different. A Russian Marxist, he was asked by his superiors in the early 1920s to prove capitalism was a failure. Instead he proposed an alternative, namely that Western capitalist economies have long-term cyclical trends of boom and bust. Mania followed by depression (i.e. they are manic-depressive). Kondratiev's theory has its critics but the cycle of boom and bust, otherwise known as 'the business cycle', is the one thing most economists do agree on, i.e. Expansion, peak, recession, trough and repeat, ad infinitum. Move along, nothing to see here folks.

What about the GD crisis calendar? Critics of generational dynamics justifiably argue that only the crises that fit the pattern are being selected (namely retro-fitting after the event), so the theory is neat at first sight but fatally flawed.

❝ *The human cognitive system identifies patterns in sequences of events, regardless of whether a pattern truly exists.* **❞** **Scott A. Huettel et al.**

As we saw in Chapter 3, there is ample scope for a healthy dollop of hindsight bias, confirmation bias and numerous other cognitive flaws to be tainting the picture. Add to this apophenia, the human condition of finding patterns where none exists and that jack-in-a-box has landed in a minefield. Or has it?

If we ignore the complexity and detail that GD throws up and just consider the disclaimer that 'it does not predict actual events but the attitudes and behaviours of entire generations', e.g. that we are prone to repeat the mistakes of our forefathers, this, alas, appears to be bordering on the indisputable. It certainly fits neatly with our many elements within the field of human psychology.

The most glaringly obvious manifestation of a repeated generational mistake is the repeal of the Glass–Steagall Act in the US. This was a piece of legislation enacted in 1933 to separate investment and commercial banking so that excessive risk-taking by banks could never again threaten the whole system with collapse following the 1929 Crash. Mmm … any of this scenario sounding strangely familiar?

In 1999 this law was effectively repealed with passage of the Gramm–Leach–Bliley Act. Disaster myopia, anyone? **What could possibly go wrong?** Give it a few years and crunch, the UK is introducing a law to separate retail and investment banking and a growing number of people in the US demand the return of Glass–Steagall. No shizzle, Sherlocks? The hilarious point within this is that Ben Bernanke, Chairman of the Federal Reserve, claimed that the financial crisis would have been avoided if there was better regulation! As we apparently say in Lancashire, *'There's nowt wrong wi'owt what mitherin' clutterbucks don't barley grommit.'* Please, Ben, my chuckle muscle has been worn flaccid, stop it: 1–0 to Generational Dynamics?

GD also predicted that the Boomer generation once in power would be overly moralistic and drive the country into crisis … mmmmmmm … done. Anyway, just to satisfy the GD crowd, number 6 in the above 'lucky' sequence of international financial crises arrived, just in the nick of time (78 years after the last one), the 2008 Credit Crunch.

> 'This is a delusion about credit. And whereas from the
> nature of credit it is to be expected that a certain line will

divide the view between creditor and debtor, the irrational fact in this case is that for more than ten years debtors and creditors together have pursued the same deceptions. In many ways, as will appear, the folly of the lender has exceeded the extravagance of the borrower.'

The above paragraph is not a recent quote, it is taken from Garet Garrett's 1932 book, *A Bubble that Broke the World*, describing the mass delusion the world suffered in the 1920s and early 1930s. Clearly it wasn't any different this time. It never is.

66 *We do not reject the 'bankers are stupid' hypothesis completely; we simply add an important nuance: they are stupid periodically.* 99 **Bill Bonner**

In fact, one could argue that the noughties had 'double, bubble toil and trouble' with both the tech and the credit bubbles occurring. Some would argue these were in fact connected and a result of central bank intervention and our Fiat currency system. It appears the first one was based on delusion, the second on fraud and, without doubt, both on greed. But after the five previous generational crashes, and numerous other financial meltdowns, **who could have seen that coming?**

DR DOOM AND THE LAW OF CONSEQUENCES

Nouriel Roubini, an economics professor at New York University, was christened Dr Doom for his presentation to the International Monetary Fund in 2006. Two years later *The New York Times* interviewed Roubini and highlighted what he had said at the time:

'In the coming months and years, he warned, the United States was likely to face a once-in-a-lifetime housing bust, an oil shock, sharply declining consumer confidence and, ultimately, a deep recession. He laid out a bleak sequence of events:

homeowners defaulting on mortgages, trillions of dollars of mortgage-backed securities unravelling worldwide and the global financial system shuddering to a halt.'

People laughed and the facilitator of the event quipped, *'I think perhaps we will need a stiff drink after that.'* Maybe they should have had more than just the one, given what was to come.

So was Roubini an eternal pessimist or permabear (as his critics would claim), just lucky, or did he simply join the dots and was clever enough to work out the direct consequences from it? Clearly he was in a minority but he was not alone. Here is what Peter Schiff, President of Euro Pacific Capital had to say in 2006:

> 'I think [the recession] is going to be pretty bad and whether it starts in '07 or '08 is immaterial and I also think it is going to last not just for quarters but for years ...'

They were voices in the wilderness (along with several dozen others). Roubini and Schiff can be accused of following the law of consequences. If you stretch an elastic band too far it will either recoil rapidly or snap completely. So quite often it's not that everyone can't see what is coming, it is more we don't want to hear bad news (we prefer to shoot the messenger). Listening to the right minority can be a wise move. The skill is identifying who they are beforehand and you can't do that unless you have a mind to.

This is how prediction of future events becomes tangible. There is a world of difference between applying some common sense to a set of circumstances and just having a wild stab in the dark. Timing exactly when events will happen is impossible but predicting their likelihood is not always that far-fetched. Do you recall the dog-kicking analogy in the Introduction? *'Are those bite marks in my leg or are you just pleased to see me?'*

THE ORGY

> 66 *I feel ya pain, I feel ya shame, but you're not to blame.* 99 **Shirley Gostman**

Let's take a moment to remind ourselves how we got into this mess. We indulged in a ten-year Orgy of Debt (prior to this was just foreplay) and now we are paying for it. Not just now but in the years to come. **Who could have seen that coming?**

Karl Marx, apparently! He suggested that capitalism would overly focus on growth at the eventual expense of the masses. However, in the race between two ideological lemmings, communism managed to get over the cliff a full 19 years before capitalism took the plunge (for more detailed 'hilarity' on what might be to come, read *Re-inventing Collapse* by Dmitry Orlov). Of course what has transpired is not actually capitalism but a highly perverted form of it. More perversion later, let's get back to the mass orgy.

In some ways at least Marx was correct, in that Western consumers have been encouraged to take on greater and greater debts, although there is a grey area between encouragement and acceptance. If someone encourages you to make friends with a lemming and jump over the cliff in a show of solidarity, would you go along with it? At the same time it's hard not to get involved if you wish to own your own house and the prices keep going up. Unfortunately it all got over-egged a tad.

If you expand cheap credit, are careless with who you lend to and don't give a flying monkey's about the long term, then at some point it's all going to hit the fan. This isn't a Gypsy Rose Lee, rub my crystal ball consultation, it's a guaranteed outcome. Most predictions are indeed notoriously inaccurate but predicting that as a race we will continue to make the same mistakes is one of the safest bets known to mankind. Patterns of the past are never guaranteed to repeat themselves but it's strange how many do.

Here is what Santa Clara University economics professor Hersh Shefrin said:

'Several factors have led to the current crisis, investment banks that excessively leveraged their debt, homeowners' finances stretched beyond their means and weak government regulation. But over-arching all of those pieces is psychology. If it weren't for psychological issues, even with all of that in place we wouldn't have the fiasco that we have now.'

Yes, it's those good ole favourite human traits we recall from Chapter 3 of overoptimism and acting like a herd of rampant wildebeest. And the cherry on the cake is greed. Anyone seen the morbidly obese cat recently?

Deregulation and fraud on a massive scale – hey, **who could have seen that coming?** Remember Mr Garrett 1930s' observation: *'the folly of the lender has exceeded the extravagance of the borrower.'* However, it was Friedrich Nietzsche who summed up this herd mentality best:

66 *Insanity in individuals is something rare – but in groups, parties, nations and epochs, it is the rule.* 99

Of course, if the Brits hadn't invaded North America in the first place it would still be run by the Native American Indians, like the Iroquois, who always asked sensible questions like, 'What effect will this particular decision have on our children seven generations into the future?' But why should we be 'scalped' by them when we can do a bit of DIY? Who needs that long-term thinking nonsense when everyone can fill their boots with big bonuses even when the company is insolvent?

66 *They loot it by destroying it but they walk away wealthy.* 99 **Bill Black**

Since when has reward for failure been part of Capitalism? Since the people at the top worked out they could get away with it? Welcome to nouveau communism, comrades.

SMACK MY BITCH UP

So clearly booms are good and busts are bad, right? The solution to the problem of borrowing too much on credit is simply to borrow more. That's why amongst other initiatives stimulus packages of trillions (US dollars, not Zimbabwean) have been initiated putting many over-indebted counties into even more debt. Confused? You are not alone. It's like giving a heroin addict more drugs as a cure for their addiction. The last time I checked you couldn't resolve the problem of being high with more drugs.

Clearly anyone with a modicum of common sense knows that borrowing is not the solution to the problem but it is a solution to another problem. To understand the issue better let's further consider the 'smack' analogy put forward by Peter Schiff to explain the business cycle:

> 'Contrary to what most people think the boom is a problem, and bust is the solution. A boom is like an artificial high like if you take heroin. You shoot yourself up with heroin and it feels really great, at least that's what they tell me. But that's artificial, you want to get healthy so you go to rehab, you go cold turkey and you go through withdrawal. The withdrawal symptoms are very unpleasant, very painful … but it's necessary if you want to remove these toxins from your system and get healthy. The same thing happens in the business cycle. When you have a central bank and the central banks make the same mistake as in the 1920s, when you have monetary policy too inflationary you create an asset bubble, you create mal investments. Mal investments need to be purged, the economy needs to be rebalanced.'

As Jim Rogers said in an interview for Barons on 20 April 2009, *'The idea that a debt problem and an excessive spending problem can be cured with more debt and more spending is ludicrous.'*

Why can't we embrace this issue? Because the boom brings the good times and the bust brings misery. It's your System 1 saying it feels bad therefore it is bad. Well, of course it can be:

> 66 *It's a recession when your neighbour loses his job: it's a depression when you lose yours.* 99 **Harry S. Truman**

As the boom felt great, it must have been great – not the source of the problem, right? It is a classic example of the **good/bad rule** in operation we saw in Chapter 3. Who on earth would vote for misery? It's like turkeys (cold or otherwise) voting for Xmas. In order to stop the misery we would have had to avoid the boom in the first place. So it's not a question of whether we can avoid the pain but only what form will it take. It's pretty much a certainty given the preceding mal-practice.

Imagine you are socialising with lemmings again and just for a laugh have thrown yourself out of a ten-storey building. You can either choose to land on your front and break all your limbs or on your back and suffer worse consequences. The *'How does this end nicely option?'* disappeared when you exited through the square window.

> 66 *He who will not economise will have to agonise.* 99 **Confucius**

When is a solution not a solution? When it's a stimulus package, of course. It was offered for several reasons, many that were not overtly stipulated:

- Doing nothing is deemed politically unacceptable. After all revolutions can be most inconvenient.

- There is a fashion for short-term thinking over longer-term solutions. Long-term solutions can be unpopular in the short term even if it's the correct medicine. Why make an unpopular decision when you can choose a popular one?

In the battle of acute versus chronic, acute is the new black. Cue massive wave of First Nation grave-turning!

- Vested interest. Politicians are more interested in re-election than doing what is right by the country. There is often a conflict of interest between the two.

- It is also easier to 'steal' money from the taxpayer, savers and future generations than those responsible.

- Oh ... and did we mention the whole economy/banking system requires perpetual growth otherwise it collapses? Better spend some more money we haven't got on projects we can't afford then?

David Einhorn from Greenlight Capital sums it up with, *'[The stimulus] has rewarded the least deserving people and institutions at the expense of the prudent.'* Or as one famous Vulcan might have said, *'It's theft, Jim, but not as we know it.'* Hey, at least it went to a good cause. As usual, this time is no different, we've been here before:

> 66 *Faced by failure of credit, they* [the unscrupulous money changers] *have proposed only the lending of more money.* 99 **President Franklin D. Roosevelt, inaugural speech, 4 March 1933**

The most scathing reaction comes from financial writer Bill Bonner, in his *Daily Reckoning* newsletter:

> 'They're squandering $13 trillion ... or nearly 49 times the US gold supply. But heck, it's worth it. The whole thing is very entertaining now ... and will be hugely instructive in the future. When this is over, the next two or three generations are sure to say: "Well ... we won't do THAT again."'

Of course, the successful execution of a stimulus package also depends on the correct allocation of resources. Capitalism in its raw form is creative destruction. Businesses that produce the wrong goods, or who are badly managed, fail and get replaced with ones that are more efficient and provide the goods and services people want. But capitalism in its raw form is exactly what we haven't had, as Dmitry Orlov points out in his 'Sermon to sharks':

> 'Throughout the world zombie financial institutions, bloated with loans which have gone bad due to a dwindling resource base and a shrinking physical economy, are gorging themselves on free government money, while the governments cannot stop throwing bags of money into their gaping maws for fear of being eaten alive.'

The above zombie feast is a gross misallocation of resources, so as we indicated at the end of Chapter 2, the diseased patient dies anyway, it's just that the process takes longer and there is a bigger bill at the end. Ouch! Would you trust a politician to correctly allocate your financial resources? With their fine upstanding principles, Wall Street connections and unparalleled fiscal probity, **what the fork could possibly go wrong?**

MORTON'S FORK

Definition: a choice between two equally unpleasant alternatives with each road leading to a different type of hell. 'Zimbabwe or Japan; that is the question,' Bill Bonner said. Niall Ferguson called it King Kong versus Godzilla. Is it inflation or deflation that matters? What is the difference and does anyone care? Well, you should care, because not only can both be devastating to your wealth, your whole investment/life strategy may need to change depending on which one it is.

There are several technical definitions of inflation and deflation and all will no doubt bore you to tears, so let's turn to the simplest definition available courtesy of James Ferguson:

'Inflation is anything that acts to bring forward spending from the future into the present [usually because goods will be more expensive tomorrow] and deflation [is anything that] acts to delay purchases from today until tomorrow' [usually because they will then be cheaper than before].

Deflation

Bad news, particularly for those with big debts. Deflation delivers a decrease in the price of assets. This means that if you have debt it is effectively increasing because whilst the size of loan you borrowed is fixed, the item you purchased is decreasing in price. Wages may also decrease which means paying off debt becomes even more difficult, especially as people start to sell assets to meet their obligations, thus flooding the market and forcing prices down even further. Japan is the modern example and that has been a basket case for two decades, but the one that is most notable is 1930s America. People living in cardboard boxes/tented cities because they couldn't repay their debts. Given the level of debt currently floating around (and it's much, much worse than any of the official figures state) the governments of the world are very keen to avoid this one, but that doesn't mean to say they can. Printing money is claimed to be the 'cure' (along with snake oil?) but what happens if you overdo it?

Inflation

Can be great news if you own debt-based assets such as mortgage-backed housing as, the effective debt level reduces over time. So inflation is good? Not quite. If you have cash savings their value will be severely eroded.

66 *By a continuing process of inflation, government can confiscate, secretly and unobserved, an important part of the wealth of their citizens.* 99 **John Maynard Keynes**

A little may be tolerable but a lot is called 'hyperinflation' and it's a disaster. Printing money decreases the value of the currency as we have already seen and makes the price of imported goods especially painful. Over to Zimbabwe, where in 2008 people could not even afford a loaf of bread because it had become too expensive.

For other examples read *When Money Dies* by Adam Ferguson. The following is an extract taken from an account by Frau Eisenmenger in Austria during 1919, a period of hyperinflation:

> 'The private tradesmen already refuses to sell his precious
> wares for money and demands something of real value
> in exchange. The wife of a doctor whom I know recently
> exchanged her beautiful grand piano for a sack of wheat flour.'

Just in case this does happen you might find a wheelbarrow and the following definitions useful:

- Trillion – 1 + 12 zeros.

- Quadrillion – 1 + 15 zeros.

- Quintillion – 1 + 18 zeros.

- Sextillion – 1 + 21 zeros.

- Septillion – 1 + 24 zeros.

- Octillion – 1 + 27 zeros.

- Nonillion – 1 + 30 zeros.

- Decillion – 1 + 33 zeros.

The problem is that no one knows what the right level of medication for the patient is. Too little and we stick with deflation, an overdose may mean hyperinflation. Extensive money printing does not always lead to hyperinflation (see Japan) but most of the time it does. The trouble is, as Matthew Lynn points out *'having a bit of inflation is a bit like having a*

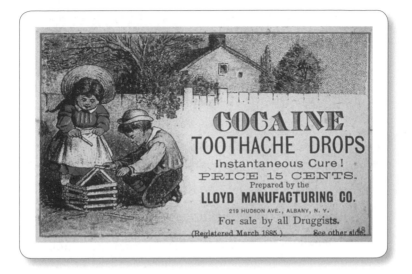

smidgen of cocaine – it's a lot easier to start than it is to stop.'
Or, as another analogy goes, it can be like tomato sauce – you
can spend ages encouraging it out of the bottle with no joy but
then a huge dollop arrives all at once.

Back to the Weimar Republic for where the pain truly hits
when inflation becomes extreme:

> 'The stupid ones were those who had nest eggs: the thrifty,
> holders of government bonds, but primarily the country's
> pensioners ... Large sections of the middle classes saw
> themselves stripped of their assets, losing almost everything
> they had set aside for years ... By perverse contrast, the winners
> of the hyperinflation were those with massive debts; first
> and foremost the state, but also private individuals who had
> borrowed money to buy houses, construction land or farmland.'

Money printing isn't a 'cure', it's another disease. Sore throat,
madam? Try two teaspoons of botulism and let me know how
you get on. So this particular 'cure' might even turn out to be
worse than the original disease. More importantly, which one is
it? James Kunstler offers a reassuring alternative:

'Some of us see both outcomes in sequence: the deflationary "work out" of bad debt currently underway – of loans that will never be paid back, of acronymic paper securities revealed as frauds … of hallucinated "wealth" rushing into the cosmic worm-hole of oblivion. Then … hyperinflation, the eraser of debt, destroyer of fortunes, and suicide pill of feckless governments.'

You can always rely on James to give the optimistic perspective. Or try this reality check from another wit:

> 66 *There will be deflation in things you own and inflation in the things you need.* 99

This may be a whole lot closer to the truth than you think. The probability of avoiding one or the other, or indeed both, looks slim. You need to be vigilant and act accordingly.

So, for example, if the disease is deflation and the cure is inflation, what does that mean for you? There will be more pointers in Chapter 8 but *if* it does play out *sequentially*, the best position may be to be debt-free initially (err … hands up who's in that position?), wait for a collapse in asset prices and then, when the printing presses truly get rolling, load up on paper (debt) and use it to buy real assets as you watch the value of paper go to zero. Alas, this is only one scenario, so the final chapter offers an insurance policy regardless of which one comes first.

That concludes our quick sojourn through the economic universe. We have seen that price and value can be markedly different. Also that housing and business cycles tend to repeat themselves and are good initial points of reference. That bust follows boom is standard business practice, and asking, 'How do you avoid the bust after the boom?' is to not understand the nature of the problem.

It's time to leave suicidal mammalian pastimes behind and instead wrestle with some grizzly livestock and, you will be pleased to know, it's a strictly lemming-free zone.

CHAPTER 6
Market DNA

Understanding how the market operates

Nowhere does history indulge in repetitions so often or so uniformly as in Wall Street. When you read contemporary accounts of boom or panics, the only thing that strikes you most forcibly is how little either stock speculation or speculators differ from yesterday. The game does not change, and neither does human nature EDWIN LEFEVRE

FANCY A COFFEE?

Getting wired on caffeine isn't to everyone's taste and neither is investing in the stock market but many people may unwittingly have exposure to it regardless of personal preference and ignorance is not always bliss. It's another area of finance that looks massively complicated but isn't, as long as you just focus on what really matters and ignore the nonsense. So in one chapter (with a follow-up in Chapters 7 and 8) you will learn most of what you need to know. To ease us in gently let's start by wetting your whistle.

Go back 400 years and all companies were privately owned by the wealthy, either as individuals or as small groups. As exploration to India and Africa got underway it became clear that a new system was desirable. These voyages needed lots of money upfront and were fraught with danger. So while the potential returns were very high, so was the possibility of the ship not returning.

These individuals did not want to face financial ruin by backing the wrong ship, so in order to buy more ships and spread the risk, joint stock companies were formed, e.g. The East India Company, which allowed the wider public to invest in them. There were no guaranteed returns but if a voyage was a success the profits were shared out amongst the original investors. This is where the term *share* originated and a share remains effectively the same today, i.e. part ownership of the assets and potential future profits of a company.

In addition, the shares in The East India Company could be sold on to other buyers at any time. As the number of joint stock companies grew, so did the number of trades and the coffee shops of London became an informal stock exchange where traders would buy and sell shares. The system was formalised in 1801 and the London Stock Exchange was created, without a 'quadruple espresso mocha choca latte ya ya' in sight.

Share prices are determined by supply and demand. One important point to make is that with shares perception is often reality. Prices often reflect what people think they are worth, not on any one set formula. We will look at one rough measure of how to value shares later in the chapter.

The alternative to shares is bonds. The main difference is that with bonds you have no ownership of the company, you are just lending your own money to the company. They promise to pay an agreed percentage in interest (the coupon) every year until your original amount of money is returned when the bond date expires. Bonds are seen as less risky than shares **but they are not risk free.**

As with shares, if the company that issues the bond goes bust you are unlikely to see your money again. Leaving the extreme cases aside, bond values normally fluctuate with interest rates. Bonds go up in value when interest rates go down and vice versa.

MEET THE SENTIMENTS

An irreverent explanation of stock market activity for the uninitiated

Imagine there is a road called Market Place (*'the Market'*). Down this street live many people. However, *'the Market'* is inhabited by two domineering families, namely the *Fundamentals* and the *Sentiments*. In fact, nothing much happens in *the Market* without their direct input. In addition there is the *Stocks* family, weaklings who have bred like rabbits for generations and now occupy most of *the Market*. But remember the *Stocks* don't own their own houses, so it's not the Stock's Market, it's a Market of Stocks. The *Stocks'* houses are owned by the *Banks*. No one likes the *Banks* (for obvious reasons).

The *Fundamentals* are the strong silent type, very powerful, conservative in nature and can't resist poking their noses into other people's businesses. They have a set of house rules covering nearly every eventuality that are to be strictly adhered to. The *Sentiments* are the polar opposites; whilst Mum and Dad are already somewhat of a random element, it is their two sons *Greedy* and *Fearful* who are clocking up more ASBOs than Vicky Pollard on steroids.

Now not only do *Greedy* and *Fearful* constantly disrupt the rest of *the Market,* there is also major sibling rivalry occurring which means they hate the sight of each other. This has led to a dramatic decision by their parents to allow only one of them to be in the house at any one time. They are hence rarely seen together.

So whilst the *Fundamentals* are trying to maintain the status quo with the *Stocks,* either *Greedy Sentiment* or *Fearful Sentiment* are running wild in *the Market* being as bloody disruptive as possible. The only saving grace is that the two *Sentiments* dislike each other so much that they always take opposite actions. So if *Greedy* builds something up, then *Fearful* goes and tears it down again. They will occasionally select a particular set of *Stocks* at random to terrorise but much prefer going after all of *the Market* at once.

Now the *Fundamentals* are a very patient lot but eventually become so annoyed they snap. Mr *Fundamental* and his twin brother *Underlying* have awful tempers and can't resist a bit of old school retribution and discipline. *Greedy* and *Fearful* will take their turn to get a good beasting from the *Underlying Fundamentals* but not before they have generated enormous stress and damage to *the Market.* So remember, the *Fundamentals* get to be in control on the odd occasion but it never seems to last very long.

There are other secretive neighbours who lurk in the background. They do not like to be seen in *the Market* so hide behind the hedge. The *Hedgies* are

1   Rich.

2   Compulsive gamblers.

In fact, their gambling habits have become so bad that they've taken to betting on which one of the *Sentiments* will be in *the*

Market and for how long. Some *Hedgies* have become even richer by making the right calls whilst others have had their houses repossessed for failing to pay their debts after borrowing too much money and backing the wrong *Sentiment*. Everyone is still giggling about the two *Hedgies* who infamously made an enormous bet that the rich German neighbours would return as usual in their Porsche but the Germans went downmarket and borrowed a VW instead … oh, how we laughed.

Finally, no one likes to talk about Uncle Madoff. He was a pretend *Hedgy* who was really a *Ponzi*. *Ponzi's* are very bad for your wealth. The only thing worse than a *Ponzi* is a *Boiler*. *Boilers* should be avoided at all costs. Most blokes say they won't touch a boiler with a bargepole but it's surprising how many still fall for a *Boiler* even when sober.

The Market has also become popular with other outsiders who cannot resist watching the Shenanigans (Irish family blighted by luck), ranging from *Day Traders* (starved cousins of *Hedgies*, who like to gamble even more but are worse at it), *Analysts*, blind as bats but can't resist telling everyone what they think they have seen, and *Journos*. Most *Journos* listen to *Analysts*, have severely limited critical faculties, change direction with the wind or tell you day is in fact night, and therefore should be completely ignored.

So there you have it, *the Market* is totally dysfunctional, with *Greed* and *Fear* running riot with only an occasional reality check from the *Underlying Fundamentals*. Easy to make money from, providing your crystal ball is fully operational and you don't do business with the *Ponzis* or *Boilers*!*

SMART MONEY VS. DUMB MONEY

We have seen in Chapter 5 that cyclical patterns exist, and the stock market is no exception. In fact, repetitive cycles are the

---

* See Appendix.

norm so it is important to understand the process and get on the right side of the market. It's time to become part of the knowledgeable, proactive minority.

> 'In financial markets, the "majority is always wrong." When the investing majority or the crowd is overly bearish, this is the best time to be buying stocks. When the crowd is overly exuberant, this is the time to be selling stocks.' (stockmarketcrash.net)

The above extract offers a useful insight into how the stock market works over a complete cycle. Think of the long-term stock market as the sea level (assume global warming and it's rising) and the bull and bear markets within it are the tides. A **bull market** is simply an extended period where the price trend moves up and a **bear market** is where the price trend is down (think 'to bear down on something' as a directional reminder). So in a bull market the money tide is coming in and during a bear market the money tide is going out. Of course, there can be big individual waves regardless of which direction the tide is going. These are the price variations and market volatility that always occur. Your focus as an investor should be on the tide direction, not the individual waves. The waves are part of the noise; the tide is where it's at. A myth that is often peddled is that stock market crashes are random events.

Tides are predictable and, to a lesser extent, so too are bull and bear markets. Clearly they are a lot less predictable than tomorrow's high tide forecast but they do occur on a frequent basis. Between 1900 and 2010 there were approximately 30 bull markets and bear markets. But these sit within longer-term up or down trends called secular bull and bear markets, each of which tend to last 15 to 20 years, and this is where we are going to focus. As Dr Spiegelhalter pointed out in Chapter 3, '*We cannot predict exactly how every precise event will turn out, but we can often predict the overall pattern of events surprisingly well.*'

The bottom of the market is when the tide has gone so far out that everyone thinks it is never coming back in: pessimism reigns supreme. At this point most investors have sold up; not

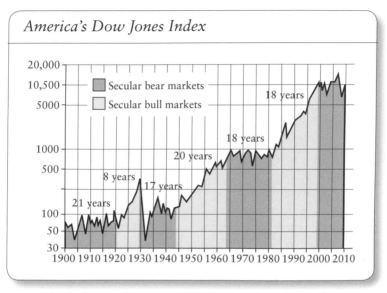

Source: Data from www.ritholtz.com/*The Globe and Mail*

only are they out of the water, they have left the beach and vowed never to return. The tide cannot go out any further because there are no more sellers. This is the point where the market is severely undervalued and where the savvy investor, the smart money, jumps in. The tide has now turned. Buying stocks at such low prices guarantees excellent future returns.

The fact that some people have jumped back into the water attracts the attention of others. More people join in and the tide of money starts to gather momentum. The big boys, the mutual funds, then pile in and the markets then advance significantly. The smart money is now sitting on some handsome profits whilst the private/retail investor is still sceptical. The markets are now getting towards fair value.

Eventually it's clear that the tide is on a roll and everyone wants a piece of the fun. Most retail investors take the plunge, wanting to catch the wave, but don't really understand what they are getting into. Investment decisions get based on recommendations from the financial press (big mistake), brokers (bigger mistake) and from tips from friends (Ouch, that hurt!). The money tide is now rising so fast that the market is soaring, leading to greed and eventually euphoria. Stocks are doubling in price and the media acts as a siren, luring people towards danger. Caution is thrown to the wind and the usual nonsense comments appear, like 'the old rules no longer apply' or 'it's a new paradigm'.

At this point the smart money sells because everything is overvalued. The smart money bought low and sold high. The red flags are waving up on the beach, but no-one is looking, people are too busy enjoying themselves in a sea of money. But the tide is set to turn. Stocks are set to go down because the market is overbought; there are no more buyers or cash left to push it any higher. The tide has only one direction to go. And as Warren Buffett famously said, 'It's only when the tide goes out that you see who's been swimming naked.' Some people are about to be left financially embarrassed. Unfortunately the tide always goes out quicker than it comes in. Those people who have borrowed money are like weak swimmers caught in a rip tide. They can be taken under before they even realise it, drowning in their own sea of debt.

However, the majority of investors don't sell even as all this is happening, believing that it is just a few weaker waves, as opposed to the tide actually going out again. Finally the tide is out over 20 per cent, sharks are seen circling in the distance and panic sets in as everyone tries to leave the water at the same time. Having been in denial that the bull market is over, now we have the mass exodus causing the tide to retreat at an even faster rate. And so the cycle completes itself. It is at this point that stocks again are undervalued. The majority of retail investors buy at the top and sell at the bottom. This is the dumb money. **Dumb money is generally not from dumb people, it's from people who are busy, inundated with bad data and are unaware of some basic repetitive patterns.**

Remember Chapter 4 and that barrage of wrong information you are constantly being subjected to? Or Chapter 3 and the misdirection offered by your primitive brain. Failure is almost guaranteed unless you do something about it. The good news is you can convert the dumb money into the smart money. It's simple but it ain't necessarily easy.

ITS BEEN EMOTIONAL

To avoid mimicking the effects of chloroform we will not be descending into a quagmire of technical diagrams, facts and figures. Let's call it the 'no reader left behind' policy. However, the odd chart can be most enlightening (visuals help) and a few simple explanations of some financial jargon will be given in order that the wider point can be fully understood. It's time for the crayons.

Markets move in cycles and are driven by sentiment over time. The image below shows how this manifests itself in

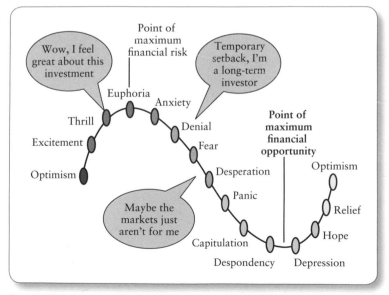

Source: Westcore Funds/Denver Investment Advisors LLC, 1998

human emotions as prices move up and down. From a low point of despair and revulsion the market gathers momentum, sentiment improves offering hope, followed by relief and a return to optimism. This optimism then builds further through excitement, producing greed and delusion, until it peaks at euphoria before then dropping back down through the negative emotions to bottom out once more. Euphoria is usually not just the top of a market but more often the top of a bubble.

According to Van Boening et al.'s somewhat dry definition, a bubble is *'trade in high volumes at prices that are considered considerably at variance with intrinsic values.'* The more humorous one being *'a bubble is a bull market in which you don't have a position.'*

We have now seen this bubble pattern repeat twice since 1999 so it should be relatively fresh in everyone's mind. The best returns come from entering the market when the majority of investors reach their max point of pessimism. This is the point of maximum financial opportunity and where the smart money wants to be.

There is another version of this figure (see opposite) which depicts the stages in a bubble that gives a little more detail and shows more accurately the level of the market during each phase.

So by anticipating and understanding the series of emotions that investors experience along the cycle you'll be better equipped to tolerate and benefit from market fluctuations. This is one of the most valuable weapons you have in your investment armoury. Like any other weapon you still need some practice in how to use it wisely, because your brain is in charge and, as we have discovered, it's not that suited to the task. Shooting yourself through the foot avoidance schemes are covered in Chapter 7.

BEAUTY CONTEST

Have you ever tried tottering around in a pair of stilettos? For the majority of women the answer will be yes, and for the

Main stages in a bubble

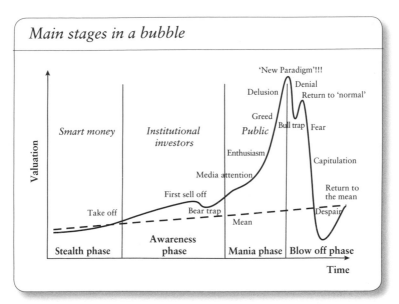

Source: Dr Jean-Paul Rodrigue, Department of Economics and Geography, Hofstra University

majority of men the answer will be 'I refuse to discuss what I do in my own free time.' They are, of course, obligatory footwear for any self-respecting beauty contestant (I'll leave the reader to decide whether that's an oxymoron).

Which somewhat randomly brings us to another analogy as to how the stock market works proposed by the economist John Maynard Keynes in his *General Theory of Employment, Interest and Money* in 1936. Keynes likened professional investing to judging a newspaper beauty contest. It's not simply a case of picking the best candidates in your eyes but anticipating what the average of the other judges believe to be best and choosing them – bearing in mind the others will be looking at the selection from a similar perspective.

   ❝ *Welcome to the behavioural freak show that is the modern investment market.* **❞ Tim Price**

As highlighted in the Seven Deadly Sins in Chapter 4, the whole market is dominated by investors who think they can out-think everyone else, although this is generally a two to three step thought process in practice. For example, if I think everyone else will visit the bank on Friday, I'll go on Thursday to beat the queue. Except I'll actually go on Wednesday because I think others will have the same idea about Thursday – I want to be one step ahead of those trying to be clever. This is all generally a waste of time but it helps to make the market perverse. **It's not about trying to outperform a specific market, it's about being in the right one at the right time.**

If you had to sum up what price a company is at any point in time in a single word, it would be **anticipation**. Anticipation of what is going to happen, or the reaction to news that deviates from that anticipation, is more influential on the short-term price of a stock than anything else. Short-term price fluctuations are like too much absinthe – they will drive you insane for no good reason. Generally it's best to disregard such meanderings but that is arguably like having a naked, prime-of-life Brad Pitt *or* Angelina Jolie begging you to come to bed (undecided readers may switch the preposition to change the proposition). Even if you don't want to, it is going to be rather difficult to ignore.

There are several types of stocks one can invest in but one should be particularly wary of growth stocks. These are stocks that are anticipated to grow their sales and profits quickly. Growth stocks are usually those of smaller companies or start ups, but not necessarily. Think Google or Apple in the late 1990s, for example. Technology is a typical sector where growth for the winners can be spectacular but there is a high failure rate to contend with so guessing the winners can be tricky. Growth stocks are not necessarily bad per se but it is because they are the most alluring that they are the most dangerous. The promise of massive short-term gains is simply dangerous bait to entrap the inexperienced.

Add to all this the fact that we think we are good at picking winners (overconfidence) and probably caught up in overoptimistic and unreliable forecasts for the future. Growth stocks are an accident waiting to happen to the average investor. Why? We tend to pay too much to own them.

66 The market overpays for future growth – relative to its ability to correctly anticipate that growth – by about two to one. The market discerns which companies are likely to do best and then overpays for those future prospects. 99 **Rob Arnott, Research Affiliates**

Growth stocks appeal more to System 1 (instinct/emotion/greed/shorter term), value stocks are more System 2 (rational/longer term) orientated. A value stock can be defined as a *stock that is undervalued relative to its intrinsic worth*. Of course, there is nothing to stop any investor looking for growth stocks that offer value, generally a far more profitable approach to growth.

Rather than focusing on growth, most investors would be better focusing on issues of greater relevance, but first we need to make a decision.

TIME HORIZONS

Whatever investments you wish to make in life there is one question you need to ask yourself before any other. When am I investing for, or put another way, what is my time horizon and how much do I need by this date? The reason this matters is because where you put your money will be impacted by when you need it back and with what return. Let's say, for example, that you were given two separate objectives:

- Double £100 in ten years.
- Double £100 by tomorrow.

In the first scenario, all you have to do is find an account paying seven per cent interest for the next decade and compound interest would ensure you double your money in the time period.

NB: One useful way of working out how long it would take to double your money at a given interest rate is the number 70. Just divide 70 by the interest rate. So for an interest rate of 7 per cent:

$$70 \div 7\% = 10 \text{ years}$$

Or, for example, if you need to double your money in certain time period, e.g. 3.5 years, just put 3.5 as the denominator and the required annual rate is given:

$$70 \div 3.5 \text{ years} = 20\%$$

In the 'double £100 by tomorrow' scenario, choices are severely limited. Perhaps a visit to the bookmakers or casino may help but both have far higher risk attached and as well as exposing you to the chance of not doubling your money, it may be that your original stake gets wiped out in the process. So, as the saying goes, the quickest way to double your money is to fold it over and put it back in your pocket.

Needless to say the stock market, and indeed most investment strategies, generally speaking are not a short-term bet. However, the mantra that *'stocks always do well over the long run'* isn't necessarily true, as we will see later in the chapter. You have to define what *long* is and what is meant by *well*, and *when* you are investing cannot be ignored either.

66 *I believe in stocks for the long run – but only if purchased at the right price.* 99 **Bill Gross**

If you take the Japanese stock market between 1990 and 2010 it's arguable the only 'buy and hold' investment worth making in that period involved a Rampant Rabbit.

ASSET ALLOCATION

Asset allocation (which sector you put your money into, e.g. specific commodities, technology, financials, etc.) is more important than stock selection within that sector. And it's not just a little bit more, it's nearly 20 times more important. Look at the following figure adapted from data in *Financial Analysts Journal* showing how asset allocation affects returns.

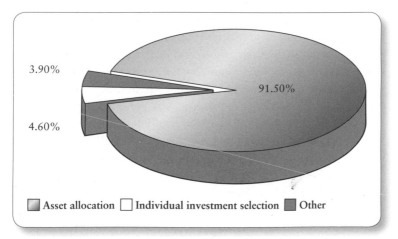

3.90%

91.50%

4.60%

☐ Asset allocation ☐ Individual investment selection ■ Other

Source: Adapted from data in *Financial Analysts Journal* (Brinson, Hood and Beebower) 1986 and 1991.

It's that classic difference between Effective and Efficient. Being in the best-performing fund in the worst-performing sector is efficient (you beat the comparables), but if you lose money then it wasn't very effective for your wealth, was it? Being in a poor-performing part of the best-performing sector will generally still give better returns. So spend more of your time choosing the sector and a little less of your time on the specific vehicle or share within it.

DIVIDEND AND CONQUER

Let's raise our heads out of the miasma for a second and reflect on where the money in the stock market is really made. Oil tycoon John D. Rockefeller once said, *'Do you know the only thing that gives me pleasure? It's to see my dividends coming in.'*

With shares you can make money in two main ways:

1   By buying them at a lower price and selling them at a higher one.

2   By receiving income from the company while owning the shares.

When a company distributes some of its profits to its shareholders it is called a dividend. Some companies don't give any, others do it infrequently. Many that do offer them do so on an annual basis and some split the payout and distribute it at set times throughout the year. How much is paid out depends on several factors and is at the discretion of the board of directors. Often the money allocated to dividend payments is expressed as a percentage of the share value of the company and would typically be somewhere between say 1 per cent and 6 per cent per annum. This is called the dividend yield. This is how much you can expect to receive as a percentage of your personal holding. You can then either take the money you receive and spend it or reinvest the dividend in more shares.

Reinvested dividends make more of a difference to your overall returns than you might think. A lot more. Why? They embrace the most powerful force in the universe, otherwise known as compound interest, that we saw in Chapter 1.

James Montier points out that the longer the time frame the more important dividends become. Over a one-year time frame 60 per cent of returns are due to changes in the share price but over a five-year period reinvested dividends account for 80 per cent of returns!

So here we have making money from shares stripped bare. In one recent ten-year period the FTSE index had made no gains without dividends but was up by 65 per cent if you included them.

If you wish to buy a stock that is yielding dividends then buy one that already is, not just one with the potential to, as history shows that promising future dividends is not the same as actually delivering them. So look for companies that already have a good dividend track record and are financially sound.

So why worry about any other approach? It's a good question. As you might have guessed, it's not without its caveats. Selecting companies based purely on dividend yield alone may be dangerous for two reasons:

1   Now you see it, now you don't: the company may decide not pay a dividend.

2   Now you see it, now you won't: the company won't be around to pay the dividend if it goes pop.

Very high yields can be a sign of distress, so the first step is to ensure companies can maintain their dividend. One measure for doing so is to calculate how many times the dividend is covered. If company earnings are £10 million and the dividend paid out is £5 million then the dividend cover is:

$$£10 \text{ million} \div £5 \text{ million} = 2$$

A figure of two and above is usually considered a good enough margin to have the dividend maintained. If it can be ascertained that the company is relatively safe then this offers one of the simplest and most effective investment strategies. Examples of consistent dividend payers include utility companies, pharmaceuticals or large oil companies. In short, don't be a divvy, go for the divi.

RIP OFF

Efficient market hypothesis (EMH) is meant to rule, OK? It is a theory that states that the financial markets are rational because trades are 'instantaneous' and buyers are fully informed, and therefore any new information is immediately reflected in market prices. It's based on the work of Harry M. Markowitz who won the Nobel Prize for Economics in 1990 – the original hypothesis was published in 1952 (how's that for proactive recognition?). Markowitz identified a method of achieving higher returns by spreading risk over different sectors. The EMH has been the accepted mantra for the last few decades but it conveniently ignores all the cognitive biases and emotions that exist within the human race. Also, buyers don't have perfect knowledge and risk in the real world does not follow a bell curve.

66 *[EMH] represents one of the most remarkable errors in the history of economic thought.* 99 **Robert Shiller**

What's more, as Tim Bennett points out in *The Great Stock Swindle*, these rational markets are supposed to funnel capital where it is best used. In truth, as Paul Woolley, ex-fund manager and IMF economist, states, '*What our financial markets are really efficient at is funnelling great chunks of an ordinary investor's capital into the pockets of an army of "agents" or middlemen.*'

Yes, folks, the system is set up to leach you dry and those impressive statistics showing how much money you can earn a year conveniently forget to highlight all the costs involved, many of them hidden. The long-term real returns have been in the region of five per cent to six per cent. But these are headline figures. Bennett points out that directors take a cut of this through share options which have amounted to 20 per cent of corporate profits, '*so you can knock 1% off that real return. Another 0.5% typically goes in merger and acquisition fees*' and

furthermore *'your broker will, on average take another 1% ...
so you are down to a return of just 2.5% to 3%, even assuming
the stock market has a relatively good year.'*

Jeremy Grantham describes stock options as *'the crème de
la crème of unjust desserts ... a legalized way to abscond with
the stockholders' equity.'* And there's more. It's like inviting
Desperate Dan around to share your cow pie, there isn't going
to be much left for you by the time he's finished taking his 'bit'.
Many funds charge you an up-front fee of 5 per cent and annual
management fees of 1.5 per cent; some will even take a charge
when you cash out. One per cent here and there may not sound
so bad but over a working lifetime it could be painful. Bennett
continues:

> 'A typical pension fund manager will trade equities back and
> forth with other fund managers with the sole effect being
> to slash the end value for a typical client by 25%, thanks to
> trading costs.'

And it's not just the financial version of Swap Shop in operation.
Unregulated and murky liquidity pools allow institutional
investors to do covert deals at prices unavailable on public
exchanges.

Dan has just taken another slice of the pie off the table.
Anything else lurking in the shadows? Unfortunately, plenty.
Recent additions favouring the city traders include high
frequency trading (HFT) and flash trading. Both employ superfast
computer programs to buy or sell before anyone else, allowing
the user with the quickest internet links and best algorithms to
benefit to the detriment of others. As a retail investor you will
not have access to these. In fact, so desperate have investment
banks become they have resorted to blowing up the countryside
in order to gain a few microseconds in speed. If you wish to take
a moment to marvel at the ingenuity of the human race watch
Kevin Slavin's algorithm lecture online at www.ted.com.

High frequency trading now represents over 70 per cent
of the number of transactions undertaken and has some of the

risk myopia hallmarks of the previous crises, in that while a few people with a brain the size of a planet can understand their own algorithms, it is highly unlikely they can understand how these black box phenomena will interact with all the other ones. So should we be worried? Yes. Are we going to do anything about it? Definitely. When? After the event of course, we are only Homo Sapiens. Slavin's conclusion? '*We are now writing code that we can't understand, with implications we can't control.*' Oh boy, this should be fun. Computer-controlled systemic risk? **Who could have seen that coming?** Anything else we need to worry about?

The exclusion of the silent evidence affects the overall market return. If a company has gone bust, then it no longer appears in the statistics. This is called survivor bias. It doesn't only apply to individual stocks, it also applies to whole stock markets that have disappeared in the past. By ignoring all the losers (the silent evidence), you make the results look much better than they actually are. Quoted annual returns are therefore overstated. You are being duped.

Finally we have further information asymmetry. The worst example of this would be insider trading and as John Kay, author of *The Long and Short of It*, points out '*just because [insider trading] is rarely discovered doesn't mean it doesn't happen.*' Regulations exist but in a battle between the City and the regulators it's the city that is usually one step in front – they pay better. As we saw in Chapter 5, all the necessary regulations existed but were repealed, often by the people who, after the crisis, then said we need more regulation. Any questions on that last point? Good. Let's move on.

So, to put the odds back in your favour you will need to follow some basic principles. Don't worry, a full list will be given in Chapter 8 once we have 'rewired your brain' in Chapter 7. Feeling reassured in a vaguely Frankensteinian manner? Marvellous. That's the cranial nurturing out of the way, now let's continue with the wake-up call. As a regular investor there are so many charges being applied to your money that even in a 'normal' market you may struggle to make any profit, as we are about to see …

WHAT'S EATING YOU?

Costs, costs, costs! Like the flesh-eating bacteria Necrotising Fasciitis, costs will eat into your savings and investments at a frightening speed and the end result – ain't too pretty.

Simon Parker was featured in *The Daily Mail* as, in 2009 after 16 years' investment, he'd made £200 more than the £34,400 he originally paid in. Ouch! Tom McPhail from Hargreaves Landsdown is quoted as saying, '*High charges ... meant many savers never stood a chance.*' We have seen that stealth charges are, unfortunately, standard practice but this level of return is a shocker. How is this possible?

Alan Miller, formerly of New Star Asset Management, has spilt the beans (albeit way after the event) declaring that fees levied by fund managers are 'disgraceful', claiming average UK costs on unit trusts are stated as 1.6 per cent but if all charges are included they rise to 3.8 per cent.

So let's just do the maths. Assuming a 7 per cent return over 45 years with no charges taken out you would receive £21,000 on an initial investment of £1,000. Now assume actual charges are 2.5 per cent and that figure reduces to £13,754. A major drop in returns.

But 7 per cent looks optimistic, so let's try a 5 per cent return over 45 years and apply the 3.8 per cent costs mentioned above and an initial 5 per cent fee. Here we only get back a measly £1,706 for our £1,000 investment over 45 years and only a £200 return over 16 years, the same as Simon received. The financial industry keeps the rest, i.e. £6,830 (assuming compound interest). The above maths example is a reworking from John Bogle's relentless rules of humble arithmetic. He concludes:

> " *So the person who put up 100% of the money and assumed 100% of the risk receives 20% of the return and the finance intermediaries who had no risk and put up none of the money get 80% of the return.* "

Allowing this to happen is well and truly being the dumb money, but the financial industry is literally banking on your disinterest and lack of understanding. The smart money keeps its charges as low as possible and recognises a delusion when it sees one: *'[The finance industry] seem obsessed with the delusion that a 7 per cent market return, minus 2.5 percentage points for costs, still equals a 7 per cent investor return,'* John Bogle.

Some good news on the horizon comes in the shape of Bogle's discount US fund group Vanguard that has entered the UK market. They work on charges as low as 0.15 per cent. Let's hope others follow suit, of course they will if they don't get any of your money because of being too expensive.

So is 'investing' in the stock market really investment or is that marketing jargon for speculation? Or is it in fact just a get rich quick scheme, at your expense, for everyone in the industry? Frankly, it doesn't matter what you call it (choose your own associated expletive) if, like Simon Parker, you are left with only a £200 profit after 16 years. This is more of a death rattle then a return. Hard to swallow?

> 66 *Consumers simply cannot grasp the fact that the man sitting in front of them and the people behind him are being paid via a long-term and hugely expensive levy on the returns from their savings.* 99 **Alistair Blair,** *Investors Chronicle*

So hopefully, how much you are giving away to the intermediaries and the impact it can have is clear.

NOTE: As per the game Monopoly, readers are now offered a chance to GO directly to Chapter 7 (on how to fight with your own brain). It isn't recommended that you do so but allows those who do not wish to drill any deeper into the stock market machinations a 'Get out of jail free' card and a short cut to some surprising revelations. For those who want to see the whole picture, and can handle a simple and essential equation, the story continues ...

LIKE SHEEP TO THE SLAUGHTER

Here is a letter from a reader printed in *The Guardian* on 8 November 2008:

> 'I read Patrick Collinson's account of the impact of the recent stock market falls on his, and many millions of other people's, pension, with great sympathy. Imagine the impact if your pension fund was nearer to £500,000 and you were about to retire.
>
> I had a similar experience during the last big stock market fall between 2000 and 2003. Then I was far too busy working to take the time to understand, fully, the risks I was exposed to and I watched the value of my personal pension plans fall by more than 20%. I naively thought I was paying fund managers to evaluate risks and make decisions on my behalf, and that the trustees would also look after my interests. On both accounts I was wrong. Fund managers for our pensions generally exercise only a limited range of discretion in their investment decisions (UK equities, corporate bonds or whatever) and their performance is consequently very similar. Like sheep, they each plod up the hill at a similar pace as markets are rising, then follow each other over the cliff like lemmings at the end of each boom. Fund managers have no incentive to act as they would if they were managing their own money, and head for safety in good times by switching funds wholly into cash for gilts prior to the fall. Fortunately I decided to put all my pension fund into cash in May 2007, earning interest at 5%.'
>
> Chris Castles, London

Without explicitly stating it Mr Castles has demonstrated a classic market timing strategy, i.e. staying out of the market in a downturn or bear market. This is a notable investment approach because you are not supposed to be able to do it. Read most of the financial press and one of the unavoidable mantras that is trotted out is, *'It's time in the market, not market timing.'*

The message is clear – trying to time the market is mission impossible and therefore should not be attempted under any circumstance. You will lose money, end of story.

'Timing is everything' according to Peter Coy, but if this is the case why aren't your friendly neighbourhood fund managers employing it or encouraging it? The answer, as we saw in Chapter 4, is that it's not in their interests or short-term bonus structures. Fund managers can't get their fees if investors are out of the market. That's why it's important, particularly during bear markets, to persuade you to stick with stocks.

As Leslie Masonson puts it in his book *All About Market Timing*, *'in most cases, failing to endorse market timing as a viable investment strategy is all about the dollars and sense of the antagonist, and not about the common sense of you the investor.'*

Vital statistics will be waived in your face, 'proving' that you will lose money by being out of the market. Probably highlighting something like this: a portfolio belonging to an investor who missed the ten best days of the market would end up, on average, with about half the balance of someone who sat tight throughout. This is true. So you would be stupid to even think about timing, right?

Tim Harford, in his undercover economist column in the *FT*, asked the inverse question: *'Why does no one ever tell you what would happen if you missed the ten worst days in the market.'* Javier Estrada gave an eye-opening reply:

> 'I established that missing the best 10 days would have reduced the return by 50.8% (relative to a passive strategy) **but also** that avoiding the worst 10 days would have increased the return by 150.4% (again relative to a passive strategy).'

So missing all the negatives has more benefits than hitting all the positives. Strange no one highlights this. But missing or hitting individual days is a nonsense that no one can deliver on. Both are red herrings … pass the dill sauce, squire.

Strategic market timing can work but it's got nothing to do with short time horizons and overactivity, as we will see later. The 'time in the market' argument is not without merit but as we have already seen, it should be linked to dividend-producing shares that can earn compound interest through reinvestment over a very long time frame, not just any old tosh.

Think about it. Here we have the financial industry being if not hypocritical at least contradictory. Take the two investment clichés:

1   'Buy low and sell high.'

2   'It's time in the market, not market timing.'

Apply this 'buy low and sell high' mantra to the overall market as opposed to individual stocks and the statement is actually supporting a market timing approach. That is, don't be in the market when it is overvalued. I do not insist that you employ it, only suggest you don't automatically exclude it.

As Warren Buffet is often quoted, as saying 'Be greedy when others are fearful, and be fearful when others are greedy', i.e. be out of a stock when it is near the top and buy back when it has dropped and most people have capitulated. But apply this to the whole market instead of an individual stock and you see the above clichés can be contradictory. If Buffett's recommendation isn't blatant support for a general market timing approach (although it is never put in this context as the quote is only ever used in terms of individual shares) then whip me senseless with a cocktail stick and call me Gertrude, but remember, for all the dumb money – *market timing doesn't work, OK?'* More on timing indicators to follow when we 'close the donut' with amongst other items, a special ratio.

THE CHARTIST MOVEMENT

Not the 18th century working class ideology but a mechanism for monitoring (and *potentially* predicting) future price movements. Charting has a lot of devotees, especially traders, and like anything else it can prove to be an extremely useful tool if utilised correctly. Many would be dumbfounded without their Candlesticks, Double Tops, Golden Crosses, Fibonacci numbers and Elliott Waves. But most of the pattern recognition involved occurs under shorter time frames which, by definition, leads to a forfeit in accuracy and, like a proverbial black hole, it is one of those fields that you can be sucked into deeper and deeper. I would like to avoid readers being put off or suffering too much paralysis through analysis. It is, however, always useful to look at the past price performance of any stock before purchasing it, if only to understand the story so far.

Those who are interested or inspired to learn more are free to do so and perhaps should start with 'the moving average' and work up from there, but one of the basic tenets of this book is that more is not always better. Certainly if you wish to indulge in some shorter-term momentum 'investing' (buying into a simple up or down trend) it is worth visiting the basics. Trading, however, is a zero sum game and therefore best avoided unless you are lucky, skilful or more to the point, both. It is often quoted that 80 per cent of people lose money trading and that isn't a set of odds I wish to bestow on you.

What is worth mentioning is the difference between so-called fundamental analysis vs charting (technical analysis), as Tim Price points out: *'Fundamental analysis focuses on "real-world" factors ... Technical analysis, on the other hand, uses charts to examine price action as a potential indicator of future direction* [and] *fundamental analysis helps you decide what to buy; technical analysis is a good guide as to when to buy it.'*

VOODOO MONTHANOMICS?

'As goes January, so goes the year' is a saying that is sometimes used to guess the direction of the market but is it reliable enough to be of any use? Well, the hit rate in correctly predicting the end of year direction is a relatively high 70 to 75 per cent depending on which market you choose. That's frankly a pretty good effort (so far) although readers should note its success rate is better in bull markets than bear ones. Notably during the Great Depression years, for instance, the correlation didn't work so well.

A significant point to make is that the January 2009 drop in the Dow of 8.8 per cent and the S&P 500 of 8.6 per cent was the worst on record. Statistics for the FTSE were similar (down over 6 per cent). At the time a pretty bad omen but one that face-planted spectacularly by the end of 2009 as it proved to be one of the more splendiferous years. Sceptics have called this less than scientific approach voodoo monthanomics. It's hard to argue against the nomenclature, and readers would be well advised not to rely too heavily on this rule of thumb.

The next bit of voodoo monthanomics comes with the saying, 'Sell in May and go away.' The idea is that you stay out of the markets between May and September and return between October and April. It's certainly true that the latter period has produced much better returns than the former but it is neither practical nor indeed cost-effective to be jumping in and out of the market every six months. Timing the exact in and out points is also an issue. We need something more reliable on which to base our decision making. Anyone feeling peckish?

CLOSING THE DONUT

I. Out and outlier

It's time to sort the wheat from the chaff. Making specific predictions only tends to encourage 'egg on face' syndrome but this should not put you off drawing some common sense conclusions from the data provided. In fact, it is essential that you do draw conclusions in order to make your own informed investment decisions. If you only look at two figures in this book, make this one:

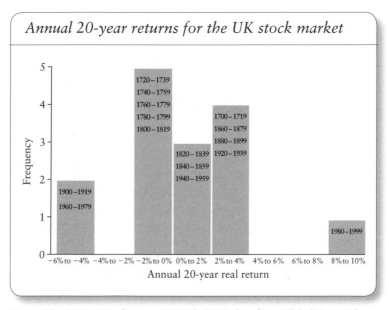

Annual 20-year returns for the UK stock market

Source: Tim Price, Newsletter no. 57, July 2009, data from Global Financial Data, Datastream

The chart shows the last 300 years of stock market returns split into 20-year blocks. As Tim Price puts it to his newsletter readers:

> 'The period between 1980 and 1999 is the only 20-year period in stock market history when the market delivered, on average, annualised real returns of between 8% and 10% per year. Those returns, over such a period, have **never** occurred before. That doesn't, of course, mean that they won't recur – but objective investors can draw their own conclusions.'

The financial industry promotes stocks because they get a percentage of your money and because by quoting the best 20-year time period for stocks in the history of mankind, it makes the investment case look much better than it really is (and that's before all those hidden costs are taken out). So, for example, a seven per cent projected annual return was often used as a reference point which is only realistic if you focus on the period 1982 to 2000.

Notice any 'recency bias' or anchoring effects here? Thought not ... bring out the beer goggles and the lipstick, there is a Leaning Jowler who wants your attention.

II. Oh-ooh, here comes the bear

Recognising the Hair Bear Bunch featured in the Hanna-Barbera 1970s' cartoon is easy. They look like bears, they have big paws, even bigger hair and they ride on top of an invisible motor cycle. Bear markets aren't quite so obvious but at least they are not invisible. As we saw earlier, markets tend to meander in long-term up or down trends called secular bull (up) and bear (down) markets, each of which tend to last 15 to 20 years with associated valuation moving from expensive to cheap. A secular bear market commenced in 2000 after an 18-year bull market between 1982 and 2000. If history repeats then the bear market may end somewhere between 2013 and 2020.

Remember, history is not necessarily a guide to the future, but as markets tend to move in cycles and rhythms, ignoring history is like shooting dead your off-piste ski guide two minutes after turning up in the resort. Just because the guide doesn't have a 100 per cent record of success isn't a reason to eliminate them completely.

III. P/E ratio

A stock price is a fairly arbitrary number and is rather meaningless by itself. It tells you nothing about the total market value or size of the firm. As a result, you cannot judge the difference in value between two companies by looking at share prices alone. For example:

Company	Share price
A	£1
B	£5

Which is worth more and which represents the best value? At this point we have no idea. Step forward the price/earnings ratio (P/E) which is a quick way of calculating how cheap or expensive a company is. There are other measures in addition to this but this is the most common. Whilst it is undoubtedly useful to understand the maths behind the ratio, so bear with it a second, it is more important to understand what the result means. First we have to know the company's total value. The value of the company (or market capitalisation) depends how many shares are in circulation as well as its share price. For these companies we have the following:

Company	Share price	Number of shares
A	£1	1,000,000
B	£5	10,000

To get the market capitalisation just multiply the share price by the number of shares. So we have:

Company	Share price		Number of shares		Market cap
A	£1	×	1,000,000	=	£1 million
B	£5	×	10,000	=	£50,000

So Company A, that had the cheaper share price, is worth much more than Company B. Now let's add in some yearly earnings for each company:

Company	Share price	Number of shares	Market cap	Earnings
A	£1	1,000,000	£1 million	£100,000
B	£5	10,000	£50,000	£50,000

And calculate which represents best value. To do this we need to calculate the price/earnings ratio. One way to do this is as follows:

P/E ratio = market capitalisation/earnings

So for each company we calculate the P/E as:

$$Company\ A = 1,000,000/100,000 = 10$$

$$Company\ B = 50,000/50,000 = 1$$

So Company B offers much better value (assuming everything else is equal) than Company A. It has a lower P/E ratio. The result essentially indicates how many years it would take to get your money back. Stocks with low P/E ratios as opposed to stocks with high P/E ratios offer better value all other things being equal. The lower a firm's P/E ratio, the 'cheaper' the stock is relative to its current earnings base.

So a P/E of three would be considered cheap and one of 30 would appear expensive. However, different sectors have different average P/E ratios so it is always wise to compare this ratio to other companies within the same sector before jumping to any conclusions. And remember, no ratio by itself is infallible. The weakness with this one is:

1   It gives no indication if a company is carrying massive debts.

2   It becomes meaningless on an individual company level if there are losses instead of profits.

Like all indicators it is best used in conjunction with others to build a holistic picture, however, the P/E ratio is still one of the most important indicators of value and can also be used to show how cheap or expensive the total market is, which is where it gets interesting.

Fortunately for the mathematically challenged there are many sources that will tell you what the P/E ratio is rather than having to calculate it yourself. Look at the P/E graph opposite for a total market (in this case the US S&P 500) between 1900 and 2010.

NB: As there is often a strong correlation between the US and UK markets we will occasionally switch between the two.

It's been as low as 5.5 and as high as 46. What is also of note is that the arrowed lines show general trends in valuation either up or down – the secular bull and bear markets:

   1900–1921 Bear

   1921–1929 Bull

   1929–1949 Bear

   1949–1966 Bull

   1966–1982 Bear

   1982–2000 Bull

   2000–20?? Bear

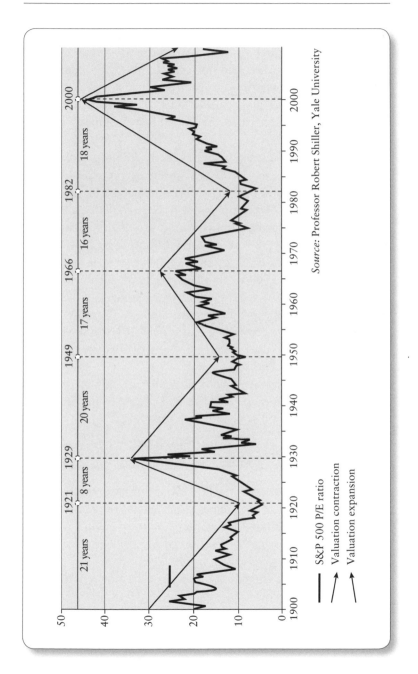

Source: Professor Robert Shiller, Yale University

As you can see, the P/E ratio has fluctuated considerably over time. We can see that it went extraordinarily high prior to 2000, all the way to 46 (the dot com bubble), i.e. completely overvalued from a historical perspective. We now have one more element coming into play, called 'the law of mean reversion'. This essentially states that markets always return to their long-term average.

The long-term average P/E has been roughly around the 15 mark. You will see a lot of talk about markets representing good value because they are at, or have dropped a bit below, the long-term average. This argument is only partially true because it doesn't include a margin of safety and it fails to highlight that in order to return to the average, the P/E must drop considerably below the average in order to balance what went before in the run up to the year 2000. It's a classic case of anchoring as we saw in Chapter 3. The reality is that markets tend to overshoot in both directions but people remain anchored to more recent price levels. We have previously had a market bottom when the P/E ratio has dropped to around 6. So if history repeats that's where it is likely to visit once again.

The P/E ratio is therefore a first port of call in trying to assess the value of any market. We will return to this indicator and what to do with it in the final chapter.

IV. Calm down

So apart from the decreasing P/E ratios is there anything else that tells us when we are facing a big bad bear? According to Tom Dyson in his 2010 Newsletter, *'Volatility is always higher in bear markets … It's a big deal when the stock market moves by more than 5%, up or down, in one day.'*

Dyson analysed the number of 5 per cent moves in the Dow Jones Industrial Average since September 1929 and found the following:

Decade	Daily moves greater than 5%
1930s*	95
1940s	3
1950s	1
1960s	1
1970s	1
1980s	6
1990s	2
2000s**	19

*Includes the last three months of 1929.
**15 of these occurred in 2008 and 2009.

So under these criteria we have had more volatility since 2008/9 than all the previous six decades put together. That's possibly significant.

Tom also notes, *'The best stock market rallies happen in bear markets. The Great Depression featured almost all of the best stock market rallies of the last 80 years'* and concludes, *'... until the volatility subsides, I'll take these rallies as confirmation of a continuing bear market and not the beginning of a new bull market.'*

Tom isn't the only one who thinks volatility is a good guiding indicator. Robert Shiller, Professor of Economics at Yale University, said in 2009, *'Recently we have been back up to depression levels of volatility'* and *'I don't know what to say about finding a bottom ... but it is a process that will evolve over years.'*

THE PEASANTS ARE REVOLTING

There is certainly an illusion of complexity and a delusion of performance when it comes to the stock market. Being a bit of a historian is a prerequisite for investing in it. Knowing exactly when the bottom will arrive is impossible to say but identifying roughly when it has should be a little easier.

Sir John Templeton once said, 'Bull-markets are born in pessimism, grow on scepticism, mature on optimism, and die of euphoria.'

Maybe we can reverse that for bear markets. They start with disbelief, drop in fear, mature on panic and die of revulsion. So at the bottom everyone will be revolting and so will the total market P/E ratio when it's in single digits.

What we do know is how long previous banking crises have taken to resolve. Kenneth Rogoff and Carmen Reinhart produced *The Aftermath of Financial Crises*, a study of 14 major banking crashes. The conclusion: six years for the housing market to recover, five years for unemployment to peak and a downturn in equities of three to four years. And let's not forget this is an *average* scenario and doesn't account for any of the tripwires we will encounter later on.

So should you even be in the market? If the total market P/E remains significantly overvalued compared to historical levels alarm bells should be ringing. Enter stage left Mr Leslie Phillips: 'I say, ding dong.' And if it's still not clear then this quote from Jesse Livermore may help:

> ❝ *In a bear market all stocks go down and in a bull market they go up.* ❞

Advice doesn't come much simpler than that. But listening to good advice may not be enough. We need to retrain the brain …

CHAPTER 7

Enter the dojo

Foible combat – retraining your brain

The first and best victory is to conquer self; to be conquered by self is, of all things the most shameful and vile PLATO

The individual has always had to struggle to keep from being overwhelmed by the tribe. If you try it, you will be lonely often, and sometimes frightened. But no price is too high to pay for the privilege of owning yourself FRIEDRICH NIETZSCHE

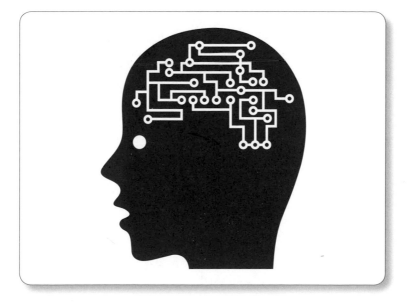

STOP FIBBING

There appear to be three reasons why most people do not get their finances in order. These I call the three FIBs, namely, Fear, Inertia and Boredom.

Fear

Is it that the whole field of finance looks complex and is therefore a bit scary? Maybe some of us feel embarrassed by a lack of knowledge or worry about feeling/looking stupid in front of 'experts'? In addition, you may be concerned about being taken for a ride. You are not alone, but being in this particular herd is not going to win you any prizes.

How did we get into this state of ignorance and fear? You have to ask why this isn't part of the mainstream curriculum at school. Conspiracy theorists would say it is deliberate and that there is an advantage to the few in maintaining ignorance amongst the many.

But hey, here in the UK there is finally an attempt to introduce lessons in money to children aged five and above, with one suggestion being tied to letting the finance industry do the educating. You can just imagine: *'and today's lesson is "how to be farmed by the bank".'* I suppose we should be making drug dealers open rehab clinics and, while we are at it, put fast food joints in charge of nutrition.

Regardless of what knowledge the system does or doesn't provide, it is time for some self-education. They don't teach you how to drive a car at school but that doesn't stop the majority of the population learning. Why? Because it is fairly essential. And your finances are exactly where on the list of importance?

Inertia

This is simply a form of procrastination, putting off until tomorrow what we could easily do today. It is a mechanism for coping with the anxiety of starting or completing a task. As Mark Twain said, *'The secret of getting ahead is getting started.'* To be honest this is a bigger problem than most will admit. Given that we are more likely to divorce our partners than change our bank account it is clear that 'pulling one's finger out' with respect to financial paperwork is not the UK's current national pastime and, unlike morris dancing and colonialism, it never was.

Life has few guarantees. Of course, death is one, and running a close second is procrastination over your finances if they are spread out over multiple providers and involve lots of paperwork. Or maybe you are in the getting started phase but haven't added the 'started' bit?

Gathering most of your investments under one umbrella which is easy to access and gives you an instant overview is highly recommended. Not only is it a cathartic experience, it's absolutely essential if you are interested in reacting quickly. But never put *all* your money in one location.

Boredom

Studies show that rich men (alpha female survey pending) who 'flash the cash' have more sex than those that don't. Is this the incentive we have been looking for in order to get our finances in order? Another advantage of sex is that it alleviates boredom. Here is a contradiction – money is sexy when we are spending it but boring when we are saving it, yet by saving it we have more of it to spend meaning potentially more sex thus alleviating the boredom generated by saving it in the first place. Those of a celibate nature and those over 100 years old may just wish to focus more on the pounds and pence side of things.

Maybe it's time to stop 'fibbing' ourselves, recognise the symptoms and take control?

The objective is to avoid being spanked and, for once in your life, it doesn't involve a paddle, a cane or a 90-degree angle.

ME, MYSELF AND I

The problem with giving your money to other people to manage is they don't care about it quite as much as you do. Perhaps, therefore, you are in fact the best person to look after it? If this appears daunting or even stark raving bonkers, the question that you should be asking is, 'Am I going to do any worse a job of it than anyone else?' Remember Mr Castle's letter from Chapter 6?

Taking responsibility for your money does not mean that you do everything alone, without help, or by completely ignoring everything the financial services industry has to offer. If you are that good then congratulations, for the rest of us there is the usual reality check and a little training required.

State of Independence may have been a high point in the career of Donna Summer but when it comes to 'independent' financial advisors (IFAs) they have been anything but. They simply pushed you into a product that:

1   Gave the biggest commission to them out of your money.

2   Was an option from their limited menu of choices.

Thankfully the situation is changing because commission-based selling is being phased out in the UK, but there are still issues to consider. Certainly the limited menu problem will still exist when you visit a tied advisor such as in a high street bank, so seeing an independent, under the new rules, should allow you to circumnavigate that lack of choice. This, however, doesn't solve the biggest problem which is, how do you determine that the quality of advice you are receiving is good or bad? I am not necessarily talking about the professionalism and qualifications of the advisors – they are all obliged to take exams to ensure a certain level of knowledge. But understanding portfolio theory is not the same as being right and being right is not always the same as making money and even that is not the same as having your best interests at heart.

Here is one litmus test you could apply: ask to see the advisor's previous recommendations to see if they meet the above criteria. For example, did they recommend holding some gold, which usually doesn't pay a commission to them (although some gold funds would) but which has been the best-performing asset class over a ten-year period? Good luck with that.

Second, you will no doubt be asked your tolerance to risk but do *they* really understand uncertainty and where the real risk is? Think back to the fingers of instability we encountered in Chapter 2. I suspect many IFAs will have a very traditional view of risk based on a bell curve. There is only one minor problem with it – it's wrong. What they have been taught is based on what has happened during a benign environment. For example, given the debt levels of some Western governments, the associated bonds (gilts in the UK, T-Bills in the US) may no longer be the safe haven that they once were – are you being told that the risk has significantly increased or is it business as usual? Do they even recognise any systemic risk or is this question received with a look of incredulity? And here's the rub, even if they do, who is prepared to step outside the expected norm? Better to be wrong with everyone else than risk being out on a limb. In the former case they get to keep their job. Remember, it's your money not theirs, and so is the risk.

Other pertinent questions could include: Are there any circumstances where they would ever recommend that you get out of the stock market? What are your expected *real* returns (and compare that answer with what you now know with respect to costs from Chapter 6) and are they just quoting the outlier performance between 1982 to 2000 as a benchmark?* You get the drift. They may have a qualification but it definitely doesn't make them bulletproof in 'the new normal'. It does,

*Most now include what happens with a 3 per cent return.

however, increase their conformity – keep asking questions until you feel you have a quality source of advice, if not, walk away.

> ❝ *Learn the basic elements of your advisor's trade. You don't have to learn very much, by the way, because if you learn just a little then you can make him explain why he's 'right'.* ❞ **Charlie Munger**

So IFAs are not necessarily a wrong choice but just blindly approaching any old advisor and abdicating responsibility is not enough. Sorry, but you are still going to have to undergo a little DIY reverse proctology ... you still need to pull your finger out. Well at least just a little so you are not an 'Ouch! potato.' Strangely enough, if you are willing to take on a little more responsibility you may have some advantages over the professional fund managers:

- Common sense.

- Freedom. You have more choice of where to put your money and you can exit the market if you so wish.*

- Time horizons. Your performance is not measured every quarter and potentially dominated by short-term thinking.

- Detachment. You are not subject to as much 'noise' and more information is not necessarily better.

- Costs. You can keep yours low using index trackers, etc.

- Cognitive biases – apply to everyone in the finance industry. They could be more susceptible than you.

---

* This is still possible even if your money is tied up in an individual savings account (ISA) as you can temporarily revert to cash (via your broker, e.g. I use Hargreaves Lansdown) without losing the tax-free status/benefits as long as you intend to reinvest at some point in the future.

❝ *Handing one's investment decisions to someone else is akin to having someone else pick your mate, your job and your home for you.* ❞ **Charles Hugh Smith**

And if the above isn't enough of an incentive, how about some extra help?

CAN'T BE ARSED FINDS THE HOLY GRAIL?

Most of us have busy lives and quite frankly don't want to spend half of them turning into financial geeks who think the *FT* is acceptable coffee-table porn. Let's face it, many of us fit into the 'can't be arsed' (CBA) category. The CBA crowd needs to find someone who is going to lighten the burden and offer the following services:

- Tells you what may happen before the event, not just after it.
- Is correct more than 50 per cent of the time.
- Is consistent.
- Has a track record to prove the above.
- Is accessible to everyone.
- Doesn't cost an arm and a leg.
- Doesn't require a degree in rocket science to understand.
- Isn't time consuming.

Finding someone who fits these criteria is perhaps like finding the Holy Grail for investment. The good news is the above criteria are met by a publication called *MoneyWeek* (disclosure: I am a subscriber but have no other vested interest in promoting it). OK, it's not the Holy Grail and won't turn you into a financial genius overnight but it does offer you an insight so that if you do choose to sit down with an independent financial advisor

it may stop you feeling like a dunce and stop you abdicating
responsibility in the face of so-called expertise. It is not perfect
(what is?) and it is not the only option but its *regular* writers
appear to pass the *'right more often than not'* test which is what
is required. What it is good at is waving red flags on issues,
such as highlighting the likely default of the Icelandic banks six
months before it actually happened, and generally defending
your capital. It's not all about maximising your gains, it's about
minimising your losses.

Everyone can be wise after the event but you want to build
up sources that were wise before a variety of events. If you had
to be the knife-thrower's assistant I trust you wouldn't choose
someone with a 97 per cent failure rate. Other sources I have
found to be both relatively independent and view the investment
world through a realistic lens (sorry, but can't name check
everyone here) include, in no particular order, James Montier
(behavioural finance), Jim Rogers (commodities and beyond),
Chris Martenson (life in general), Bill Bonner (history and
reckoning), James Turk (golden insights) and the ubiquitous
'Tyler Durden' at ZeroHedge.com.

A big question for many people if they choose to invest in
the stock market is, 'Do I invest in funds or individual shares?'
There is a major danger with individual stock selection and that
is fraud/surprises that appear far more often than they should –
especially after a long boom. If you go for individual stocks then
you need a range of them and a selection process that doesn't
involve just guessing.

On the flip side, with individual shares, unlike funds, you
are not paying annual charges (see TCO, below) which is a
massive incentive in their favour. You pays your money and
takes your choice. Funds still make sense for many people but
only if you can get your annual costs down low enough and it
generates an acceptable level of return (see Chapter 8 for some
more context).

If you choose to invest in a fund, do try to obtain in addition
to its headline performance a *total cost of ownership* (TCO).

With fund fees there are essentially three levels of charges: the annual fee, e.g. 1.5 per cent. This is what everyone focuses on and most people believe represents their total cost, but isn't – there are other hidden charges. The total expense ratio includes other costs you are subject to but not the *total* cost as the name implies (remember you are dealing with the finance industry here). The TCO includes **every** cost (including the administration charge) which is the figure you really want to know (if they will allow you to have it). As Merryn Somerset Webb points out, you don't go into a supermarket to buy your shopping to then find out you have been charged more than the advertised price once you have left the building, regardless of whether or not your name is Elvis. We saw in Chapter 6 how devastating these hidden charges can be. Not containing them may mean a zero return or worse. A good target is to get costs below one per cent per annum. Not that difficult if you look at index trackers, exchange traded funds* (ETFs) or fund groups like Vanguard.

> 66 *Most investors will find the best way to own equities is through an index fund that charges minimal fees. They are sure to beat the net results (after fees and expenses) delivered by the majority of investment professionals.* 99 **Warren Buffett, 1997**

With respect to taking responsibility I am assuming there will be two camps: the ones that want to take full responsibility

---

* **NB:** with many ETFs you are not the official owner of the underlying asset even if it is backed by something physical. They are also subject to nonsense words such as 'rehypothecation' (the underlying asset being lent out to third parties) and therefore these may not be suitable in a crisis, especially as the underlying asset can be lent out multiple times – fractional reserve loaning … surely not? Before investing you need to ask one question: 'Show me the counterparty', i.e. who owns the underlying asset and what happens in a worst-case scenario? An insurance policy only works if the insurer does not go bust. And lastly, be careful with commodity ETFs. Many don't do what they should and can drop in value even if the underlying asset has increased in price over time. But we digress …

and those that want to partially abdicate it. Full abdication is
not an option unless you particularly like 'flogging a dead horse'.
It may appeal to the equine branch of the BDSM club but it will
do little for everyone else.

Whatever you choose, sooner or later you are going to be
making investment decisions or deciding who will make them
on your behalf. And whichever camp you reside in there is some
self-awareness training that is recommended. In this arena you
get to fight with yourself, or more specifically, your brain. As
Bill Bonner puts it, *'We're far more beholden to biology than
we think.'* The biggest hurdle to overcome is not the market but
your own behaviour.

BRAIN REWIRING

Is there actually any point in trying to fight your natural instincts
if many of these are hard-wired into our brains? Rewiring a plug
is apparently a challenge for some people, so rewiring the brain
might be one step too far. Is it even possible?

Well, as usual with your brain, it's a good news/bad news
scenario. The good news is it's not impossible, the bad news is it
isn't easy either, and it can take a long time.

If you want to be inspired by determination in the face of
adversity, you can do worse than read the story of Cheri Florence
and her son Whitney in *A Boy Beyond Reach*. Whitney was
considered a deaf mute from birth. Doctors diagnosed him with
autism, and with an IQ measured at only 49 it was suggested
he be placed in an institution. Fortunately for Whitney, his mum
was a renowned brain specialist who set about confounding just
about everyone by rewiring her son's brain.

Cheri Florence broke the unwritten rules about professionals
not treating their own family, jeopardised her professional
credentials and had school psychologists file complaints about
her. It took a minimum of eight hours a day and relied on
Whitney's siblings' full involvement in the gargantuan task.

The result: one broken marriage, one mended son, a very happy family unit and a complete change in our scientific understanding of what is possible. Whitney's IQ was reassessed at the age of 16 and found to be 150, high enough to join MENSA.

As the more observant may wish to point out, spending eight hours a day with a brain specialist and two siblings you may or may not have in order to try and rewire your brain is a little OTT. Can't it just do it by itself? Well, it can if your name is Terry Wallis, whose brain 'spontaneously' rewired itself during the 19 years he was in a coma after a severe car crash. He has now regained his speech by growing tiny new nerve connections. The network of brain cells seemed to reform at a glacial rate but in doing so have *'shaken the foundations of science, causing neurologists around the world to revise their notions on how the human brain functions.'*

Clearly both these cases are extremes but demonstrate what is possible with even severe disabilities. Most of us are fortunate enough to be in a much better starting position than either Whitney or Terry. Is there a possibility that we can alter our thinking?

Rewiring is a little like walking through a cornfield in summer. Walk the path once and one can just pick out the trail. Walk it several times and a visible path emerges. Keep walking the same path on a regular basis and it becomes stronger and clearer until that becomes the main route. As we know, practice makes perfect and if we are going to try to battle our instincts then we have to practise. This ability to mould our minds is called 'plasticity' and that means exercising a few behavioural muscles...

FIGHT CLUB

In Chapter 3 we saw why one of the biggest hurdles to successful investment sits in your cranium. Frontal lobotomies are neither convenient nor desirable and far from problem-free, so 'retraining' the brain is the only realistic option. The idea of the dojo* is that we focus on those specific areas that most affect our investment decision-making and whilst fully rewiring your brain is light years beyond the capabilities of this text, at least if you are aware of what forces are at play you've a better chance of catching them. One can only try. The aim is to fight your natural instincts. It is time to enter the dojo.

Opponent 1: Fear

This is the largest and ugliest opponent. Fear distorts your thinking and makes you take actions that are often repented at leisure. It tends to make you either freeze up (do nothing) or alternatively makes you cut and run at the wrong moment. Fear is also 'ambidextrous' – it gets you with a left on the way down and with the right on the way back up. Markets can be rising but fear stops you getting back in if you have chosen to jump out. It comes in two formats, fear of loss and fear of the unknown.

Few of us are ever going to beat this fear in a fight so the only alternative is to try to make friends with it. Fear brings opportunity and value and knowing that fear's appearance is scaring everyone else into irrational behaviour should offer some comfort. But fear is very powerful so just talking about it is not enough.

You need to be able to let emotion wash over you so you know what it really feels like. In practical terms this means going through the actual experience of buying when everyone else is selling in a panic. Olympic athletes visualise winning, and as an investor one should visualise buying when all those around you are selling. Then when it happens, you have to put it into practice. You need to feel the fear. It's quite hard to do but usually rewarding.

> ❝ *If an investment feels 'comfortable', then you are probably too late.* ❞ **Anthony Bolton**

* Dojo – a martial arts training room.

Looking to buy when no-one else wants to often offers the greatest returns in the long term, be it stocks, housing or anything else. Perhaps one could apply a rule to only invest when it is uncomfortable to do so. Take comfort in the fact it should feel uncomfortable!

One fear mitigation tactic is to keep an emotional investment diary. Write down how you felt when you made an investment. If you can see over time that your best investments were when you felt the most fear and worst when you were the most confident/euphoric then you can try to train yourself to use your future feelings as a reverse indicator.

And don't forget the background fears we have already encountered such as the fear of getting started and the fear of taking responsibility.

> ❝ *Confidence comes not from always being right but from not fearing to be wrong.* ❞
> **Peter T. McIntyre**

Opponent 2: Pain

Following hard on the heels of opponent number 1 is pain. Remember how social exclusion is felt in the same part of the brain as physical pain. It is much easier to go along with the herd. But if you agree that the majority are usually wrong then it is in your interests to do the opposite.

> ❝ *Value investors are the financial equivalent of masochists.* ❞ **James Montier**

Look for strong consensus of opinion and then remind yourself that this is a valid signal to jump off the bandwagon even if the ride feels fantastic – in all probability the wheels are going to fall off at some point in the not too distant future.

Opponent 3: Loss

Humans are loss averse. We feel a loss at least twice as much as an equivalent gain. This leads to some irrational behaviour, as we saw in Chapter 3. This can manifest itself in several ways.

● Reluctance to invest after a loss.

● Refusal to sell when a price drop has occurred until at least break-even has been achieved on that selection.

● Taking higher risks in order to compensate for another loss elsewhere.

Studies of investor behaviour by Meir Statman, Finance Professor at Santa Clara University, show that *'losses bring sadness, disgust, fear, regret. Fear increases the sense of risk and some react by shunning stocks.'* We become paralysed as we suffer smaller losses.

As we saw in Chapter 3 in the experiment betting on a coin coming up heads or tails on 20 occasions, few people took the rational approach to invest in every round.

Taking the second point, not crystallising (taking) a loss is a widespread disease amongst investors.

❝ *Everyone is looking to get back to break even after a loss ... taking a loss is basically admitting to yourself that your judgement was wrong and that you failed as an investor.* ❞ **Leslie Masonson**

Try to overcome this issue by changing your perspective. Imagine you are in a race to Glasgow with ten others and the last one to get there will be shot dead. Think Mad Max meets Frankie Boyle ignoring the national speed limits. There are 20 cars to choose from but to make it interesting the engines have all been swapped around and the bonnets welded shut.

The race gets underway and you realise the Ferrari you have selected has the engine from a lawnmower under the bonnet (most items look good at the point of purchase but some are inevitably going to disappoint). Do you hold onto the botched Ferrari in the vain hope it might be a temporary blip, just to see it fall further and further behind, resulting in last place and guaranteed death? Or do you accept you made a wrong decision ditch it and go back to the start, picking another car which will probably get you there much quicker even though you have lost some ground initially? In this ludicrous example, avoidance of death makes the decision much clearer but the principle applies to poor-performing investments. The question is, can you apply it in practice?

The answer back in the real world will depend on the circumstances. Don't stubbornly stick with something that under current circumstances you wouldn't buy again. The loss that has been realised allows you the opportunity to reinvest in something that is working and get your money back more quickly (provided it is not another lawnmower in supercar clothing!) And this action shouldn't affect your previously agreed risk level. Under emotional distress people shift to favouring high-risk, high-payoff options. Don't chase the loss with high-risk gambles.

So if paralysis stops us selling shares when prices are dropping, why at market bottoms have most people sold? One word – disgust. Small and medium losses create negative feelings but with major losses it is much harder to accept our own bad decision making. Loss aversion switches to incompetence aversion. Better to remove the reminder of our ineptitude and wipe the slate clean. Our memories are great at erasing the losses and remembering the wins – but only if it's not staring at us in black and white.

Opponent 4: Inconsistency

When buying or selling you should decide on a price and stick to it. The problem is that as the price changes we are very much tempted not to fulfil the original agreement we made with ourselves.

This is the empathy gap problem we met courtesy of the self-gratification class of 2005 at 'The University of Californication.' Just as the students were willing to compromise their morals when aroused, investors are willing to compromise their previous decisions when under the emotional pressure of buying/selling. When we get to the actual moment of the decision, we can behave differently from how we said we would. Even prior knowledge of this fact does not necessarily alter our behaviour, and it's not just a male trait either. For example, Montier highlights that *'92% of women reported that they knew that condoms were useful in preventing HIV/AIDS transmission, but only 63% used them!'*

Be honest with yourself. Use non-negotiable rules as a cut off when buying/selling to help overcome this inconsistency. Also remember prices may appear cheap after a drop but only when compared to the previous price. Compared to long-term historical values they may still be expensive.

Opponent 5: Linearity

Humans have a tendency to see the future as a linear extrapolation of the immediate past. This leads to wildly inaccurate expectations and forecasts, especially at major turning points. Traits such as anchoring amplify this problem.

Scott Huettel et al. from Duke University performed an experiment where participants were shown a random sequence of squares and circles, for example:

●●■●■■●■●●●● ■

Amongst the discoveries made was the brain's anticipation of a pattern as soon as two or more repetitions occurred. For example, after ■■ we expect another ■.

Jason Zweig, author of *Your Money and Your Brain*, having extracted this information eloquently ties it together with a previous observation from Benjamin Graham: '*The speculative public is incorrigible. In financial terms it cannot count beyond 3.*'

This may explain why investors sometimes pile into sectors that have performed well over the last two years. They are pre-programmed to expect the sequence to continue. We seem to be looking for a ménage à trois! The market, however, behaves in a cyclical and somewhat random fashion, not always a linear one. Talking straight is definitely more important than thinking straight.

Opponent 6: Impatience

Humans are pleasure-seeking creatures and we have our own inbuilt cerebral drug factory to ensure we get what we want. Various external triggers can generate a release of dopamine into our systems to give a natural high. It has even been shown that just performing the physical act of smiling can make us happier. The physical action triggers the release. Being some sort of natural junkie may be appealing but it also has its dangers, particularly when we try to align short-term benefits with long-term gains.

Remember the analogy of the boxing match between System 1 and System 2:

66 *We have different neural systems that evolved to solve different types of problems, and our behaviour is dictated by the competition or cooperation between them.* 99 **Steve Bradt,** *Harvard University Gazette*

In the red corner we have emotion and in the blue corner, logic. Logic is fighting on behalf of delayed gratification and emotion is fighting for that short-term dopamine hit. Seconds out, round one:

'*Our emotional brain wants to max out the credit card, order dessert, and smoke a cigarette. Our logical brain knows we should save for retirement, go for a jog, and quit smoking,*' says David Laibson, an economist in Harvard's Faculty of Arts and Science, '*our emotional brain has a hard time imagining the future, even though our logical brain clearly sees the future consequences of our current actions.*'

The majority of dopamine receptors are found in System 1, emotion and instinct. So System 2, rationality, is already at a disadvantage. Impulsive actions are known to trigger dopamine-related circuits in the brain. But what does this mean in reality for investors, especially as monetary rewards also trigger the release of dopamine? A research paper on delayed monetary rewards by Samuel M. McClure et al. states that:

> '[*Investors tend to*] behave impatiently today but plan to
> act patiently in the future. For example, someone offered
> the choice between $10 today and $11 tomorrow might be
> tempted to choose the immediate option. However, if asked
> today to choose between $10 in a year and $11 in a year and a
> day, the same person is likely to prefer the slightly delayed but
> larger amount.'

Investment is about long-term decisions but we struggle to resist the short-term temptations. This is why the Lottery is so appealing. It's a drug deal.

So what to do if you class yourself as a dopamine junkie? There have been studies showing that in general woman make better investors than men because they are more cautious, trade less frequently and don't seem to need the quick hit of a big short-term gain. Women were shown to deliver 1.4 per cent per annum better performance in a study by Barber and Odean (both men, incidentally, and the sample size was 35,000). Why women should be less inclined to need the short-term dopamine hit when investing, given that their reputation precedes them when it comes to shoe shopping, probably comes down to perceived risk of each particular activity. Women, as a rule of thumb, appear to be more risk averse.

This approach sums up the Fight Club mentality. If you can't eliminate your internal opponent at least try to temper the threat level. Outright victory in every battle is clearly impossible but by succumbing to your emotional biases in a limited way, perhaps one can limit the overall effect. So if we return to the radish and resistance example (Chapter 3) instead of, say, eating either only radishes (healthy, logical, long-term choice) or chocolate and cookies (naughty, emotional, short-term choice), why not eat mainly radishes and have a cookie on the side? That's the biscuit, not my Australian friend Cookie – Cookie Nookie is off the agenda; she has already been impregnated.

In terms of investment this just means splitting your money so that the majority goes into the logical and boring choices with longer time horizons and a small minority of your money is reserved for the emotional, racy and fun options. Want to be more aggressive? Be defensive and aggressive. By accepting you can't resist temptation completely you behave in a more rational manner with the rest. 'Proper job', as they say in Bristol.

Opponent 7: Overconfidence

Nothing fails like success! Investors should perhaps leave the radishes, chocolate and cookies to one side and focus on eating as much humble pie as possible. We think we are 'better than average' (competency bias), highly skilled (self-attribution bias) and are permanently wearing rose-tinted eyewear (optimism bias). Remember the drivers, 70 per cent thought they were better than average?

Made a right call? Perhaps luck rather than judgement was the reason? Never get too carried away by investment euphoria. Victory rolls should be reserved for fighter pilots. Complacency and overconfidence have a nasty habit of biting you somewhere around the gluteus maximus.

Opponent 8: Obedience

There are those that obey and conform and those that don't. If you went through the standard educational system then you have had years of brainwashing in the art of conformity. The danger is that even those 'low self-monitors', who by definition are not that interested in what others think of them and do not show much deference to figures of authority, will often still listen to those who are perceived as experts in their fields. It is not that experts should be completely ignored but the tendency to switch off your critical thinking ability when faced with someone who *supposedly* knows more than you could prove expensive. Don't accept anything at face value without verification, even experts and IFAs are not good at navigating uncertainty.

Take solace in the fact that it usually only requires one dissenter to break the spell of conformity. Why can't that be you? Once one has spoken, others who thought the same will then speak more freely. If dissenting feels too difficult, try starting with a healthy dose of questioning. Question everything – much less scary, but just as effective in finding out if the expert is right.

There is a tendency within corporate structures, including the finance industry, towards homo-social reproduction. This isn't a gay sex procreation phenomenon but rather an unconscious desire to promote those that conform and fit in, thereby reinforcing the type of behavioural traits that already exist, and woe betide those that don't. It may be good for people's comfort zones but isn't necessarily good for the overall health of the company or your finances.

66 *I think the reward for conformity is that everyone likes you except yourself.* 99 **Rita Mae Brown**

Opponent 9: Risk appetite

Base jumping involves throwing yourself off a cliff or bridge or maybe even a hotel roof and hoping your parachute opens before you splatter on the ground. It's an extreme sport which involves a considerable level of risk and as such has a limited number of participants. It will come as no surprise that some people are much more risk averse than others (that's personality for you) but what might be more of a surprise is how our individual attitude to risk varies depending on our mood. Your attitude to risk is not fixed, it is variable. Understanding this will hopefully make you a better investor rather than a metaphorical participant in a roadkill look-alike competition.

There have been numerous experiments to show how our emotions affect our behaviour at any given moment and how we try to overcompensate for what has gone before. For example if we feel embarrassed we are then much more willing to adopt risky strategies in order to rectify the situation. We observed the changes when people were aroused. Press the right buttons and people are more likely to shun contraception, i.e. display more risky behaviour. On the flip side, if we feel anxious or sad we are much less willing to take risks. So your risk tolerance changes over time.

Try to recognise when you are in a heightened emotional state and compensate accordingly. Being emotionally neutral at the point of investment is preferable but it's not quite as simple as that. Often a good time to buy is when you are feeling the most anxious, and conversely if you feel like you are missing out this is usually a good reason not to buy.

Chapter 3 highlighted several reasons why risk is poorly understood. We suffer availability bias and recency bias, and from the good/bad rule. Although as Warren Buffett said, '[Real] risk comes from not knowing what you are doing.'

When it comes to investing, the following risk pyramid (based on John Exter's inverted original) may be helpful but none of the investments are risk free.

The investment pyramid

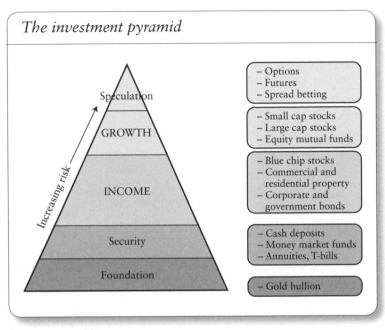

Source: www.gold.ie

The diagram shows the pyramid split into different levels, with risk increasing as we rise up it. Whether Western government debt still deserves its allocated position from a risk perspective may be up for discussion. It may prove to be 'the go to asset' in the short-term but would you lend your money to a bankrupt with a gambling habit?

Opponent 10: Greed

When it comes to relationships it is often said that 'the fun is in the chase.' Could it be that anticipation of a reward is more relevant than the actual receiving of it? Further elements to be considered include the alliteration factors – the 'reward relativity' and the 'size of surprise'. Knowing how our brain rewards us and under what circumstances is an important step in controlling it.

Never has there been greater pressure to be rich than now. Comparison with others plays a huge part in this process. With the advent of the internet, on top of already being bombarded via other consumption-driven sources, we are constantly reminded of what others have that we don't. Subsequently this drives the desire for more, it makes us greedier. In the drive to acquire more, risk and reward are correlated. Let's return to the risk equation we met in Chapter 3:

$$\text{Risk} = \text{consequence} \times \text{probability}$$

You recall how our brains focus on the consequence part, processed by system 1, and it is left to system 2 to work out the probability. Now let's replace general consequence with monetary reward, so it reads

$$\text{Risk} = \text{reward} \times \text{probability}$$

It's now the 'reward' part of the equation that gets our attention. This part we can intuitively feel, the probability part is more abstract. But here is the thing – the brain is much more sensitive to changes in the size of the reward than changes in the size of the probability. The bigger the reward, the bigger the distraction and the more likely we are to fantasise about receiving it.

People are likely to invest more in the Lottery when the jackpot is larger even if their chances of winning it are lower. Greed takes over or, as Jason Zweig puts it, '*When possibility is in the room, probability goes out of the window.*' But it's not just about the size of the prize, it's the size of the surprise that counts.

Some readers will recall the 1999 European Cup Final between Bayern Munich and Manchester United. Bayern

Munich were leading 1–0 from an early goal as the match went into injury time.

It's fair to say that at this point the Bayern fans were happy, expecting a win and were starting to celebrate accordingly and the Man United fans were resigned to the loss (although with hindsight bias some may deny this). The win for Bayern looked assured. Manchester United then scored twice in injury time to win the game.

Instead of 'happy' and 'disappointed' we witnessed 'euphoria' and 'utter devastation' as the expected result reversed. This is the size of the surprise. Surprise rewards are felt with a greater explosion of brain chemicals than expected rewards.

Having won big, this then becomes imprinted on/burned into our memories much more clearly than a small win. And just like a junkie we want to recreate the feeling again and again. This explains why, after receiving so much attention and adulation, ex-pop stars are so willing to embarrass themselves on celebrity TV shows to try to repeat the feelings generated by their initial fame.

Winning big in terms of a lottery win or making a huge amount of money on a risky stock is addictive and therefore dangerous, especially if the first time was down to luck. You are highly likely to want to repeat the experience but the outcome isn't necessarily going to be the same.

Start to marry greed with higher risk and the issues become more exaggerated. We get a greater buzz from successfully investing in something where the downside is larger than in receiving an equal amount of reward from something that is low risk. This is reward relativity. Greed in this case is as much about feeling clever as it is about being rich.

Perhaps what is most surprising is how your brain gives you little reward for receiving what you already expect. Hans Breiter at Harvard Medical School said, *'Reward is experienced in two fundamental ways,'* arousal and satiation. According to Shultz at Read Montague, *'Getting what you expect produces no dopamine hit.'* And Emrah Duzel concludes, *'the anticipation of reward ... is more important than the reward.'* As suspected, 'the thrill of the chase' is not an illusion, it seems it is often the prize.

We are more aroused by the anticipation of a stock rising than when it actually does. This may account for some of the more bizarre fluctuations in prices we see occurring. This partly explains why when good news is delivered prices go down or vice versa. Meeting expectations is not good enough. The action is in the anticipation and that's how the market works.

So 'Opportunity Knocks' for the private investor who can successfully challenge this last opponent, but don't forget 'Opportunity Remorse': feeling sick that you missed out on a big gain, which then tempts you to throw caution to the wind. It's another form of greed that will hoist you by your own petard.

So what does this all mean in practice? Jeremy Grantham sums it up in one of his quarterly newsletters:

> 'If you can be patient and ignore the crowd, you are likely
> to win. But to imagine you can, and then to adopt a flawed
> approach that allows you to be seduced or intimidated by the
> crowd into jumping in late or getting out early is to guarantee
> a pure disaster. You must know your pain and patience
> thresholds accurately and not play over your head. If you
> cannot resist temptation, you absolutely MUST NOT manage
> your own money.
>
> On the other hand, if you have patience, a decent pain
> threshold, an ability to withstand the herd mentality, [an
> understanding of basic maths], and a reputation for common
> sense then go for it. In my opinion, you hold enough cards and
> will beat most professionals (which is sadly, but realistically, a
> modest hurdle) and may even do very well indeed.'

And with that wise advice under our wings we now need to ensure no one is eating our prehistoric money metaphor ...

CHAPTER 8

Who ate my mammoth?

Avoiding extinction and riding the money tides

I'm not so much concerned about the return on my money, but the return of my money WILL ROGERS

We cannot let other people do our thinking for us A. BARTLETT

BARKING MAD

> 66 *We have two classes of forecasters; those who don't know, and those who don't know they don't know.* 99 **John Kenneth Galbraith**

Mmm ... time to return to the Introduction; kick the dog (proverbially speaking) and guess what happens next? This isn't so much prediction, it is action and reaction. Indeed, if our Fiat currency system were a modern four-legged friend, given the abuse that has already been dished out to it, not only would our 'dog' be howling like mad but the RSPCA would have been called in years ago. But that doesn't mean it can't get worse before it gets better.

To recap, we face a dilemma because the system under which we live has not only been abused but is itself fundamentally flawed. If you are still not convinced I suggest you watch the film *Four Horsemen*. We now get to enjoy the consequences that are, unfortunately, unavoidable. It is only a question of *how* you would like to accept the pain, as if you have a choice in the matter. Well, maybe you do, in that you can choose to prepare or not. It's actually a classic asymmetric risk mitigation situation. Errr ... run that one by me again? OK, just ask yourself, what's the downside of taking action and being wrong versus the downside of taking no action and being wrong? The first may be a minor irritation and the second, financial extinction. Or put more simply, low probability, high impact scenarios are a bummer, especially when the low bit is no longer that low. Insurance policy, anyone? Readers would also do well to heed the following:

> 66 *In a depression, the winner is the person who loses the least money.* 99

So is it the barking mad dog, our mammoth or a T-Rex we should be worried about?

METAL GURU

Every time mankind has managed a zombie-bloated empire and stolen too much wealth from the future it's not ended pleasantly and one antidote has usually involved owning something that is yellow and shiny.

Gold has little or no 'utility' apart from the minor fact it has been used as money by humans for over 5,000 years and, unlike the paper currencies, there is a strictly limited supply. It's this last point that provides its 'utility', one yardstick that has been accepted over the millennia as money and doesn't wildly vary with time. After all, there is a reason why the SAS have gold coins, as opposed to paper, sewn into their belts and why the Chinese government has legalised precious metal ownership and is telling all its citizens to actively invest in it. Although the astute will notice gold's lack of edibility can be a problem in a *real* crisis.

One often quoted sage (of Omaha) certainly isn't feeling the love:

> 'Gold gets dug out of the ground in Africa, or someplace.
> Then we melt it down, dig another hole, bury it again and pay people to stand around guarding it. It has no utility. Anyone watching from Mars would be scratching their head.'
> Warren Buffett, Harvard, 1998

I'm not interested in winning an intellectual argument with a proven financial guru, I'm concerned that your savings don't follow Phineas Gage's frontal cortex, way out West, and get blown to smithereens. If governments choose to monetarise debt (print money to meet debt obligations) the most likely outcome is severe weakening of the currency or, in a worst case scenario, the destruction of paper currency in its current form. Gold, and don't forget silver, will hold its value, i.e. go up in price. It's history vs a great reputation. Whilst I'm willing to acknowledge genius I'm not willing to bet against government mismanagement and mathematics.

> ❝ *Gold is a speculation. But it is a*
> *speculation on a certainty: the debasement*
> *of the currency.* ❞ **James Grant**

Those people who want to bury their heads in the sand are also making a choice, they are just choosing the size of pillow they are compelled to bite! The secret to protecting or even increasing what you have is knowing the rules of the game you are inadvertently playing. Of course, being invested in the right things at the right time matters – and this varies with the tides. Let's go for a swim.

MONEY TIDES

As we saw in Chapter 6, asset allocation (which sector to put your money) is 20 times more important than individual stock selection. For example, investing in gold in 2000 was wise, *how* you invested in it was far less relevant. Whether it was in physical bullion, stocks or an exchange traded fund* – all performed better than the stock market or property over the following decade. Quite simply, asset allocation matters and by association so does some form of timing. Short time horizons give a much higher level of unpredictability. Consistently guessing the correct direction of a market in the short term is a skill few people possess and helps to explain why trading is so difficult, and unprofitable for the majority. It is in fact a zero sum game and that's before you take away the costs. The longer the time horizon the simpler the patterns become.

There are thousands of individual investments you can make but only a few main categories. Cash, shares, bonds and tangibles (land, property, commodities, etc.).

---

* See previous warning comments on ETFs in Chapter 7.

Modern Portfolio Theory suggests a diversified approach will give superior returns. This has been technically true but there is a system that may give better ones. Surf's up, dude – it's time to ride the money tides.

In Chapter 6 we discussed the market being like a tide. Waves are short-term price movements and just a distraction; what is important is whether the tide is going in or out. Are you in a long-term bull or a bear market? Now, each investment class has its own tide and its own tide table. All you have to do is to be aware of that and be able to read it.

These tides are not absolutely fixed time periods but they are not totally random either. We touched on the property cycle in Chapter 5 and the stock market cycle in Chapter 6. Put in simple terms, these are the money tides. Just ride the right ones at the right time. Impossible? Not really. It's simply a buy low and sell high routine with a long time horizon. The difficulty isn't necessarily recognition, it's also being able to act on it.

Let's look at an example (see figures on page 188) with gold and the US Dow Jones Index. If everything went up and down in value together there wouldn't be much to say, but that's not the case.

Gold has generally performed well during times of financial mismanagement – 1930s' deflation*, 1970s' inflation and the noughties' money debasement extravaganza. When gold is going up shares have generally performed badly and vice versa. At the moment it is gold's turn to shine and then, when it has fully revalued, it will peak and then it will be time to get out and look for another tide to come in.

One could also widen this argument to commodities in general and, hey presto, we get the Commodities Supercycle. These are periods where commodity prices rise – it's another secular bull market and often occurs when stocks are in a secular bear market.

* via gold mining stocks.

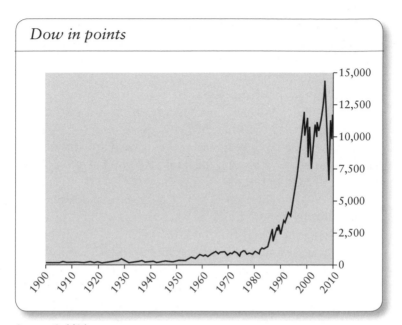

Source: GoldSilver.com

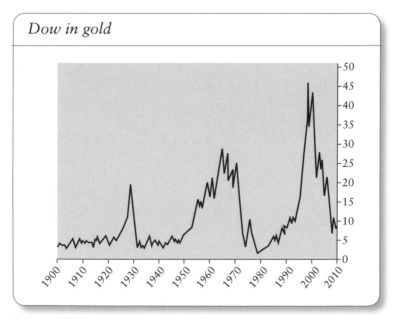

Source: GoldSilver.com

Let's look at the data using gold and stocks. What would happen to your money if you were able to ride each money tide at the right time over the past 100 years or so as opposed to just sticking with stocks? Michael Maloney, in his *Guide to Investing in Gold and Silver* suggests the following:

1903 – 1929 Stocks.

1929 – 1932 Gold.

1932 – 1966 Stocks.

1966 – 1980 Gold.

1980 – 1999 Stocks.

1999 – 20?? Gold.

Using this system Maloney suggests the difference is eye-watering. Not switching and staying in stocks offers a substantial reward: US$30 turns into an impressive US$12,000 – well, at least it looks impressive until you realise that by switching it turns into US$11 million!

This looks easy, except it isn't. Picking the points of inflexion in **hindsight** is easy, doing it at the time isn't. So US$11 million is a little disingenuous as a target figure but even though hitting the exact switch points is not going to happen (that's called hindsight bias) being aware that these patterns exist should allow you to be in the ballpark once momentum starts to build, i.e. it is still going to be very worthwhile riding the tide. It's 'simple' asset allocation.

Overleaf is a similar suggestion from Grant Williams between 1970 and 2010: Gold, Nikkei, Nasdaq, Gold. This would have turned $35 into $224,000.

Same 'gotcha's' apply here (needs a healthy dose of hindsight bias to work) but it is another more nuanced play on riding the same tide.

This shouldn't be an all or nothing approach but it does allow you to intensify your investments in the relevant incoming tide and reduce your holdings in the area where the tide is going out. In

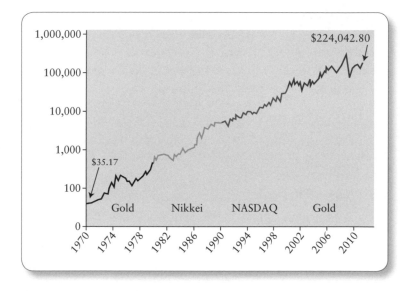

order to save ourselves from drowning most of us learn to swim. Financially speaking, are these money tides any different? Putting all your eggs in one basket looks like a genius move in hindsight but if, in the unlikely event the future refuses to reflect the past, only having one basket is going to look like the 'very dumb money' not the 'smart money'. On the flipside, only putting 10 per cent of your savings into a bull market (the suggested maximum percentage you often read about with gold) is somewhat missing the point about where the danger actually lies. As Marc Faber points out:

> **❝** *Owning gold is not the risk... not owning gold is to trust the government.* **❞**

Disclosure: On a personal note I have been invested in precious metals since 2006 purely because the gold (and silver) tide is coming in, but like any other tide it will peak and then it will be time to move into another asset class. The next obvious question is, 'Are there any metrics to suggest when this may occur and at what level?'

To my own disappointment, as much as anyone else's, I still don't own a functional crystal ball but last time gold peaked at 24 times its starting point (a multiplier metric). In the two months prior to its high point it doubled in value (a rate of increase metric) and reached a level where 1oz of gold was equal to the total level of the Dow Jones Index (a value comparison metric). Gold started at $35 and peaked (very briefly) at $850. This peak today, if adjusted for inflation, would be in the region of $3,000 per oz. Or a lot higher if you use John Williams' 'shadow stats' figures for inflation (www. shadowstats.com) as opposed to the 'Mickey Mouse' official ones.

Silver is generally far more volatile than gold and last time increased by 36 times its starting point. The low point this time for silver was $4 and for gold $252, which would, if history were to repeat exactly on these multiples (and 'exactly' never happens) end up with silver at $146 and gold being valued at $6,000 per oz.

Next we have a volatility metric as highlighted by Jeff Clark at Casey Research. He points out that the price of gold and silver will become more volatile as we near the price peak. In 1980 gold rose by 13 per cent in one day and 19 days later a drop of 13 per cent signalled the end of its bull run. As for silver its highest one day rise was an eyebrow-raising 36 per cent and its biggest fall was 18 per cent. He concludes:

● If history repeats, or even rhymes, our biggest days of volatility are ahead. And they will be normal.

● Big price fluctuations will be common as we enter the mania and approach the peak.

Of course *this time* it would not be surprising to see *much bigger* price swings.

Another way of looking at it is to view gold as a percentage of US currency in circulation (another value comparison metric).

As this time there is a much larger amount of paper money, if gold returns to parity with the number of dollars in circulation (like it has twice before in the 1930s and 1980) it would be beyond $10,000 per oz.

Impossible? No, not at all; it went up to over 140 per cent of American paper in 1980, but don't hold your breath on that

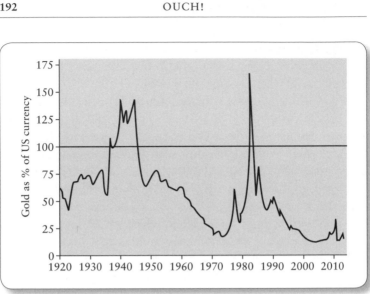

Source: GoldSilver.com

figure and I certainly wouldn't use this as an anchor (although as we know from Chapter 3, now I've mentioned it the damage is already done).

Finally, as we saw earlier, we have gold measured against the Dow and there are several people betting we will see parity again (or even an overshoot) between the two. Of course this may just mean a horrendous drop in the Dow as opposed to gold shooting to the moon.

Silver is far more volatile than gold in price (if you can't handle a 60 per cent short-term fall then don't touch it) but the upside is potentially far greater. The planet has approximately 17 times more silver than gold but has often traded in a range between 40 and 80 times less than gold, although it briefly dropped to its planetary ratio in 1980.

What is of particular note is that the industrial uses for silver are expanding almost monthly. The amount available for investment purposes is surprisingly less than gold as much is used in manufacturing and is not investment grade, and it also suffers from depletion due to non-recycling. Being a smaller market it is therefore subject to wilder swings. A recession usually kicks it in the teeth temporarily.

It's certainly not one for the faint hearted but more extreme views here include levels of $300 per oz and beyond. James Turk has pencilled in a possible $400 for silver and $8,000 for gold. And in the very long term, if silver ever reaches parity with gold you will be seeing a few more people joining *The Lonely Island* boys singing, 'I'M ON A BOAT!'

Hold up a second, isn't this one boat that's already sailed? Isn't too late to be investing in precious metals this time around? Yes, the easy money has gone, but it's still got to complete its journey and the fact that denial still reigns and ownership levels are relatively low means opportunity still exists. The question that is often asked is, '*Aren't gold and silver in a bubble?*' Actually, we do have a huge bubble but it is in paper currency, not yet in gold and silver. That's a key point to take away. What is also imperative to understand is that all of the above dollar priced metrics are somewhat meaningless as price is a function of how much paper money is printed. It's that elastic yardstick again and if it's stretched to ridiculous lengths then the gold and silver prices will be too to reflect that fact – so please don't take any of these figures as gospel they are purely to give some historical context. Further, historical charts/metrics may no longer give accurate clues to future movements if demand totally outstrips supply. The last time gold and silver prices erupted neither the Russians nor the Chinese were involved. There will be a lot more people chasing the stuff this time round.

Let's assume for argument's sake gold and silver are in a bubble. Bubbles, as we know from Chapter 6, have three long-term phases before they pop. Stealth, awareness and then mania (see 'Main stages in a bubble' figure on page 131).

If gold is in a bubble then what you are watching out for is the mania phase, as media attention transitions through enthusiasm/greed/delusion and euphoria. You will know it's in a proper bubble when all your friends are fully invested in it and you hear people saying 'gold never goes down'.

For the final word on when to sell it's back to James Turk. He suggests when gold peaks *'you won't need to sell it, you will just have to spend it'* (i.e. in his opinion at some point it will once again be *officially* recognised as real money). Could this all not come to pass? Of course, but it would be wise to hedge your bets in case it does. *Physical* gold and silver being your safest bet. If you do wish to invest in physical gold bullion via professional vaults there are online options but I suggest selecting those that offer *allocated* gold and issue a daily audit list (I use bullionvault.com).

Money tides vary with time but can also be geographical. A good example is Sam Zell who, as one of the world's largest property tycoons, sold out of the US just before the crash in 2007 and invested in Brazil. Why? Well, apart from the fact they do a good line in coconuts and caipirinhas, Brazil was near the bottom of its credit cycle and the money tide was starting to come in, whereas in the US at that point the tide was high – and 'holding on' was a *Blondie* lyric, not a sensible investment position. But don't forget the advice from the investment industry: *'Market timing doesn't work!'*

So the secret is to know when an asset class is overvalued and switch to one that is undervalued. These asset classes generally take years/decades to build up before unwinding so it's not something you need to think about that often. You do not need to know precisely when the tide is turning, just when an asset class is overvalued and when it is undervalued. Of course, one should add the caveat that if a totally foolproof strategy did exist then everyone would use it, thereby negating its advantage. As this is a long-term (System 2) strategy, as opposed to a short-term (System 1) strategy you can be fairly certain many won't indulge. It's not exciting enough.

We have touched on the metrics for gold, what about the anchor points for shares and property?

WEIGHING THE ANCHOR

What is value and when do you know whether something is good value or not? We may be clear about this when it comes to everyday household goods but what about the stock market. Fortunately it's not that complicated if we return to the price/earnings ratio (P/E) we encountered at the end of Chapter 6. (NB: if you used your *Get out of jail free* card it might be worth having a quick peek back.)

P/E is just an indication of how many years it would take to get your money back. So a P/E of three means it would take three years of earnings to get back your investment at the price you paid. It's the most basic and reliable measure of whether the market is cheap or expensive. Remember, no stand-alone formula or ratio can give the whole picture but P/E has proven itself to be one of the most reliable over long timescales. Let's bracket them as follows:

0–6   Cheap as chips.

6–10   Undervalued.

10–15   Fair value.

15–20   Overvalued.

20–30   Expensive.

30+   Bubbles, darling.

If you recall, these P/E ratios vary over time, so now let's insert the actual P/E over the last 100 years:

Sell above 20 and buy below 10. Of course, by following this advice you would not have maximised your returns between 1995 and 2000 as P/Es went from 20+ to nearly 46, but obviously they didn't stay there. One should also note that different sectors have different P/E ratios but we want to keep it simple, so here we are looking purely at the total market.

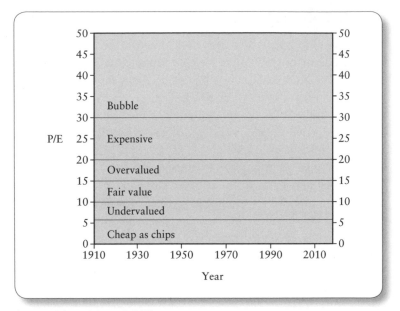

Source: Adapted from GoldSilver.com

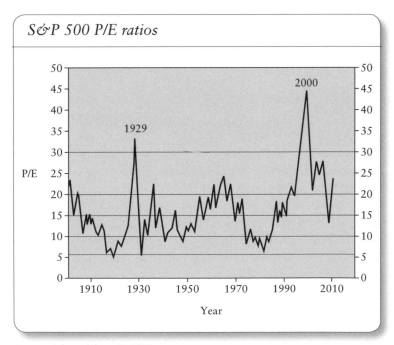

Source: Adapted from GoldSilver.com

Be very wary of comments such as: 'The market is fair value, so now is a good time to invest.' Every time the market has hit a peak it then goes on to hit a low trough. Who wants fair value when you can get it undervalued or, as is likely, 'as cheap as chips'? Fair value is just selecting a better but still far from perfect anchor point because what you really want is a margin of safety. You want some lardy chips with plenty of salt and vinegar.

Remember, P/E is only one ratio and never gives an indication of debt levels. It is also a meaningless figure if a company isn't making a profit but used in the above context it's effectively a financial Carlsberg advert, 'Probably the best indicator in the world'.

Another simple metric is to use dividend yield. The higher the yield, the better the value:

0–1%   Forget it.

1–2%   Expensive.

2–3%   Overvalued.

3–5%   Fair value.

5–8%   Undervalued.

8%+   Cheap as chips.

Jim Rogers was quoted in *Fortune* magazine as saying:

> '*Historically, you buy stocks when they're yielding 6% and selling at eight times earnings. You sell them when they're at 22 times earnings and yielding 2%.*'

Well, that seems pretty clear advice. The only question is, do you have the patience for this approach and can you act on it?

What about property? If you have to buy in the UK due to personal circumstances (giving birth to octuplets may be a valid excuse) then timing when to jump in may be irrelevant. If it's you who will be living in the property, unlike other investments there is a quality of life issue to consider before any other. But let's put that aspect to one side and look at housing purely from an investment perspective. We met the three rules of property investment in Chapter 5 but what are the best metrics to assess value? We have two that have proven to be the most reliable *over the long term*:

1   The ratio of average house prices to household wages.

2   Rental yield.

The first ratio is a measure of affordability but one that has accounted for periods when there were higher interest rates. House prices have averaged approximately 3 to 3.5 times household wages over the long term but have overshot (and undershot) this figure by a considerable margin. It has recently been over 6.

Rental yield is defined as the annual rent divided by the cost of the property expressed as a percentage. So if a house costs £100,000 and it generates £10,000 per annum in rent it has a 10 per cent yield (this is a gross figure before costs are removed). Or put simply, how many years rent does it take to get back your original investment? A gross yield of 10 per cent would be considered healthy (depending on interest rates) but it's what it produces after all costs are taken out (net yield) that really matters.

Rental yield is a good indicator of true value as it extracts the emotion from the situation and puts the price of property in true investment terms. Why put your money into property with, say, a 3 per cent yield when you can get the same return elsewhere and without all the hassle of tenants and repairs? The only argument for doing so is if prices are rising (or there are no other options!). Low rental yields are often an indicator that property prices are historically high.

When you're enjoying an ultra-low interest rate environment you just need to remember there's no cast iron guarantee it will remain like that forever. Even if rates remain low house prices can still fall in value, as Japan has proven. There is always reversion to mean value at some point, regardless of the ridiculous props sometimes employed to stop this from happening. Of course, there is one guaranteed way to temporarily distort house prices – start printing loads of money and sell lots of prime central London property to foreigners who think it's a safer investment than the overly reproductive pound sterling or their own doomed currency.

Be clear on which metric to use and know when it represents good value. In other words, anchor to the right point. These are the technical valuation indicators but we have a second set and they are the emotional anchor points and are just as reliable.

As you recall we go through several emotional states over time as markets rise and fall. The figure in Chapter 6 (p.129) offers a road map. The best time to buy is when the outlook is at its worst and everybody is depressed or repulsed by that investment category.

The smart investor doesn't need to be a financial genius, they just need to combine some simple technical indicators with the key emotional indicators **and then act on them** when it's time to do so. As we will see, it may be in your best interests to puke up before you buy …

THROWN IN THE STOCKS

> 66 *The market will do whatever it can to cause the most pain to the most people.* 99

Throwing rotten apples and putrid vegetables at the shackled used to be a run-of-the-mill activity in olden times. Public '5-a-day' retribution for erroneous behaviour provided hours of fun for the great unwashed – even the deliverers could be confident of being slightly cleaner than the receivers by the end.

Jumping into the wrong stocks in modern times will be a more monetary affair but perhaps the 'old school public humiliation method' is preferable to having your investments bear no fruit at all. It is frustrating reading about normal investors, like you or me, reporting that after x years (fill in your own length of time) their investment is worth less than they have put in.

This shouldn't be surprising; it should almost be expected because the finance industry has become so parasitical it is killing its hosts. On top of that, not only are we in a secular bear market (and if you believe Mauldin and Tepper, at the end of a massive 60-year debt supercycle, with some lovely consequences) but also in an asymmetrical environment where the odds are stacked against us. We have seen how statistics are skewed; there is unseen survivor bias, and much anchoring by the finance industry to outlier returns which are not representative of the current environment. Costs are higher in practice that actually quoted, stock options to employees take returns from investors, and few normal investors have access to 'guaranteed' anomaly trading advantages such as high frequency trading. In short, we are being leached by a parasite. What is clear is that just putting your money into an overvalued market isn't big and it isn't clever. I can't know the direction of the market, no one can, especially with rampant money printing artificially manipulating it, but I can recognise when I am not willing to fully participate – for all the right reasons. I demand some value.

If you are of the disposition to indulge, here, for your delectation, is what I call 'The Not So Dirty Dozen'. A reminder of the 12 principles/rules to abide by, using what we learned from previous chapters, in order to put the odds back in your favour:

1 Get a margin.

2 Ride the tide.

3 The Sloth is King.

4 WTF is going on with quantum entanglement?

5 Eat some chocolate.

6 I hate Crowded House.

7 Puke up and buy.

8 How low can you go?

9 Yield now, Sire.

10 Check yourself, before you wreck yourself.

11 Unrequited love.

12 Ignore the sirens.

1. Get a margin

Look after the losses and the gains look after themselves. Insisting on a margin of safety is, according to James Montier, the first immutable law of investing. He explains: *'Valuation is the closest thing to gravity that we have in finance.'* You shouldn't just be looking to buy at fair value but actually below it – include an extra buffer. This is your margin of safety. Use the relevant anchor points (e.g. market P/E ratio) and make your own mind up whether something offers good value or is 'as cheap as chips'. Most people quoting it is a great time to buy have a vested interest in your money, not a good grasp on reality. It may be wise *on occasions* to sit on cash and wait for the right opportunity.

2. Ride the tide

Some people choose to bash their heads against a brick wall. If it is part of your religious etiquette then you may have a 'good' reason for doing so, otherwise it's a waste of brain cells. So why not ride the money tides rather than trying to swim against them?

> ❝ *In a bear market all stocks go down and in a bull market they go up.* ❞ **Jesse Livermore**

The simple rules work better than the complex and asset allocation (which sector or market you put your money into) matters more than individual stock selection, so focus more of your time here.

3. The Sloth is King

Temperament trumps intellect. Patience is something that is in short supply so employ it to your advantage if you are able to.

> ❝ *It never was my thinking that made the big money for me. It always was my sitting.* ❞ **Jesse Livermore**

The more you check your shares, the more you are likely to trade, therefore *infrequent* reviews are an essential tool in your armoury. Less is indeed more.

Riding any bull market is going to test your temperament. A lack of patience also increases trading costs and lowers returns.

> ❝ *Much success can be attributed to inactivity. Most investors cannot resist the temptation to constantly buy and sell.* ❞ **Warren Buffet**

NB: Sleep may not technically count as patience but when it comes to inactivity the Sloth is the King. For the truly lazy, don't forget – being a Sloth after taking the appropriate action is good, being one due to inertia in the first place isn't. And neither is abdication of responsibility. The Sloth is a poster child of your patience, not your laziness.

4. WTF is going on with quantum entanglement?

I don't know either. Don't invest in something you don't understand. But do understand this – if you make a good call don't get overconfident or cocky – it may just have been luck.

5. Eat some chocolate

Take 1 per cent of your money and invest it in something on a whim you know nothing about, were given a tip for, or fancy for no particular reason. Resistance is futile – the more you resist the less you are able to, so why not accept you are weak, especially if you are a bloke,* and do it anyway. 'Man' cannot live by radish alone and succumbing to the cocoa bean, as many women already know full well, may be in your best interests. Just make sure the chocolate bit is only 1 per cent of your money and no more. And when it all goes horribly wrong just frame it as a reminder of your own rank stupidity. This should protect the other 99 per cent to use in a sensible manner.

6. I hate Crowded House

An irrational dislike for an Antipodean pop phenomenon or just a sensible investment position? When no-one else can get in, then it's already time to have left the party. Don't get greedy and wait until the end to sell. 'The trend is no friend at the end.'

> ❝ I got rich by leaving the last 20 per cent to someone else. ❞ **Anon**

Be a contrarian – the majority are nearly always wrong in the investment world and if you can't be one yourself find someone who is.

---

* Women appear to be more risk averse.

Find out what the **most popular** investment idea for the year is (NB: this is not necessarily the best performing – it takes time for people to notice), then blatantly ignore it. As Brian Hunt in the *DailyWealth Newsletter* highlights:

'Subscribers wanted internet stocks in 2000 (80% crash) … China in 2007 (70% crash) … and oil in 2008 (72% crash). It's just human nature. People tend to go crazy for the same ideas at the same time. In finance, this kind of crowd mentality produces horrific catastrophes for investors … Wall Street is never shy about releasing investment vehicles hundreds of percent too late.'

'You're either a contrarian or a victim' as investment guru Rick Rule puts it, so don't be afraid to go against the crowd even if it is painful.

7. Puke up and buy

Use emotions as a contrary indicator. General Revulsion is not a video game, it's a buying opportunity. Use the emotional cycle to help time the tides. The Sentiments rule the market.

❝ *If it makes me feel like I want to throw up I can be pretty sure it's a great investment.* **❞** **Brian Posner**

The difficulty here is the empathy gap conundrum we encountered in Chapter 3. Saying what you will do and actually doing it in the heat of the moment are two different things. Herein lies the opportunity but by definition not everyone will be able to take it.

8. How low can you go?

Not to be mistaken for a drunken limbo challenge after the tenth rum punch in a Jamaican shebeen, but rather a wise note of caution over costs. As we have already seen in Chapter 6, the finance industry is there to make sure it gets paid first, which means your initial pot is going to be eroded before you even get started.

It is therefore your sworn duty to keep your costs low and not to let the finance industry take huge amounts in fees, either overt or covert.

9. Yield now, Sire

You are a genius and can second-guess every stock movement? For everyone else why bet against the facts.' **Reinvested** dividends account for most of the returns over the long run. It's simply our old friend compound interest at work, and guess what? It does. Buy some current yield and then, like a bad dose of eczema, leave it well alone.

If you want to boil down a yield strategy into one short summary try this: P/E tells you when to buy and dividend yield* (as long as it's maintainable) tells you what to buy. Compound interest and good cost control do the rest.

10. Check yourself, before you wreck yourself

Understanding risk is not our forte as human beings. Never forget to diversify. That doesn't mean invest in as many things as you can think of. It means investing in a number of sectors you believe will perform and if possible are non-correlated (do not rise and fall in sync). It means spreading your risk but not so thin that you don't have a significant position in anything. Remember Buffett's observation: *'Wide diversification is for those who don't understand what they are doing.'*

What you certainly have to avoid at all costs, as Benjamin Graham warned, is a *'permanent loss of capital'* – aka fiscal extinction. No diversification, no sympathy! It's that simple. If

* See Dividend and Conquer (Chapter 6).

you put all your money in one location and lose it, do yourself and everyone else a favour – stand away from the gene pool.

The elephant in the room with respect to investment is that there can be a gaping chasm between the theory and actually applying it in practice. Sayings like, 'Sell your losers and ride your winners' abound, but at what point do you actually know that loser is an absolute dog or just a temporary setback before it shoots through the roof or vice versa? The reality is that in the short term you don't, there are just too many variables involved.

But 'Ride your winners and sell your losers' is generally sound advice and a mantra of choice for trend investors. The majority of people find it incredibly difficult to sell something they have lost money on but are also too quick to sell those stocks that are in profit. Why? It's your friendly neighbourhood ego interfering as usual and if you are not careful, it can wreck you.

Selling a stock at a price below what you paid for it involves accepting you made a mistake. That means taking two losses, a financial one and a psychological one. No one likes to do this so instead we sit and wait for it to improve. What makes it even more difficult to sell is the fear of repeating the mistake. A mistake that results from affirmative action is much harder to deal with emotionally than one resulting from inaction. It's the difference between being a loser and just losing out.

11. Unrequited love

'Objectum sexuality' is the official term for falling in love with an inanimate object. Just make sure it's not your stocks and shares as it will only lead to disappointment. You could try the Berlin Wall instead – although one lady might object:

> 'Eija-Riitta Berliner-Mauer is married to the Berlin Wall.
> Like any couple, they've had their ups and downs, but over
> the years, they've been able to meet each other's spiritual
> and emotional needs. "We even made it through the terrible

disaster of 9 November 1989, when my husband was
subjected to frenzied attacks by a mob".'

If the criteria or reason why you bought has fundamentally
changed then it may be time to admit when you are wrong
and sell. Don't cling on for old times sake. It might have been
good while it lasted but nothing lasts forever including, alas,
you.

Endowment or ownership of an item makes us think it
is worth more than it is, or certainly more than others who
don't already own it. Being well endowed is not necessarily an
advantage in the investment world.

12. Ignore the sirens

Think, 'How much could I lose?' not, 'How much could I
gain? Stories are for bedtime ... not your portfolio. There is a
compelling argument for every single investment on the planet.
It's called a sales pitch ... a particular nasty contagion in the
financial world.

Want to buy a stock? Ask not what the finance industry can
do for you but what you can do for the finance industry ... then
slap yourself across the face with a wet fish for a massive reality
check. Ignore the sirens, it's not the police after you this time, it's
the light-fingered pickpockets of fiscal enlightenment.

Watch out for all the cognitive disorders and issues such
as 'framing'. Find some good sources of information with a
decent track record, not just the most convenient. Much that
appears in the mainstream press is old news. Get ahead of
the curve and question everything. Think about your inbuilt
cognitive biases we first met in Chapter 3. For example, if you
have to anchor to *something* make sure it's the *right thing* and
don't react to the latest news without balancing it with what
has gone before.

Also remember the old stock market adage, 'Where there's
a tip there's a tap' and, as P. T. Barnum once said, *'There's a*

sucker born every minute.' Never get persuaded into buying stocks or shares from a cold caller. And finally, history suggests linear extrapolations of the present are not the best way forward.

So where to put your money becomes the 64 million dollar question. Well, the answer to that depends on many factors and whether you have any in the first place.

We want to put the odds in our favour so as well as pursuing 'The Not So Dirty Dozen' principles we want to make an informed decision on whether the tide is coming in or going out.

After a long period in a bear market, history says shares are likely to return to a severely undervalued status (as they always have after being substantially overvalued) and therefore it's sensible to wait for that to happen before getting too excited. That doesn't mean to say they can't go up before they go down. Take Eric Kraus's immortal words:

> ❝ *If you pump enough liquidity into a corpse, it will get up and walk – pump in more still, and it will dance; that does not mean that it has Fred Astaire's career before it.* ❞

So staying away from an overvalued market until it tanks looks like a no brainer – especially with 'invisible' systemic risk lurking in the background. If most of your money is in the market, then where are you going to find the funds to invest when gravity kicks in? Oh, that's right, you'll be so disgusted with the amount of money that has been lost that you won't want to go near it with any bargepole, never mind yours. The finance industry would like to thank you for believing all their marketing hype, embracing 'conservative bias' wholeheartedly and behaving exactly as expected.

> ❝ *We are single-digit years away from the most profound market clearing moment.* ❞ **Hugh Hendry**

At some point of course it will look so bleak it will be time to pounce. Will you be wise enough to act before, or bold enough afterwards?

> 66 *There will be a time when you believe everything is finished. That will be the beginning.* 99
> **Louis L'Amour**

Many people will think their portfolio is balanced because it is spread between different shares and bonds. Not only should Western government debt (bonds) come with a health warning, but if all these investments are in fact 100 per cent paper assets you might want to embrace your inner lemming. This may be diversification masquerading as a financial suicide mission.

> 66 *If you're going to lend your money to a country (which is what buying its bonds represents), it makes sense only to lend to those countries that can afford to pay you back.* 99 **Tim Price**

Investing in tangible assets as opposed to paper ones is the best investment advice there seems to be although this is hardly a new concept:

> 66 *Buy land, they're not making it anymore.* 99 **Mark Twain**

But you may wish to preface the word land with 'farm' or 'wood' especially if hyperinflation is ever allowed to get underway. Although in these radical circumstances stocks (not bonds) usually perform well too. Here is an observation made by Lion Feuchtwanger about the 1920s' German experience, courtesy of *Der Spiegel* magazine: 'Most farmers also did extremely well. "They had money to burn, and spent it willy-nilly".'

Or a more up to date recommendation:

❝ *Become a farmer. Finance is finished.* ❞
Jim Rogers

There is, of course, another investment sector that is worthy of merit, if only because it's quaintly subversive...

FROM PEER TO ETERNITY

❝ *In the end, if bankers take us to the cleaners we mainly have ourselves to blame.* ❞
Tony Jackson, *Financial Times*

Maybe it is time to cut out the middleman? Peer to peer lending (sometimes called 'social lending', 'person to person' or 'P2P') is a new investment category and one that is growing substantially.

It works by cutting the banks out of the equation.* The individual who is the lender is now effectively the bank. Unlike the banking model, you cannot get interest on money you don't have, but at least you can get good interest rates on the money you do have to lend. It also provides a genuine diversification for any investment portfolio.

The system works by linking up individual borrowers and lenders. While some offer direct one to one lending, in order to lower the risks your money should be spread amongst a number of borrowers, i.e. on a many to one basis. So, for example, if you lend more than £500 it may be spread across at least 50 borrowers. By diversifying who you lend to, you lower the risk of default. It's no good earning ten per cent per annum interest if your original capital evaporates after the second year.

The attraction of this model is threefold:

---

* Peer to peer lending still uses a banking institution to facilitate transactions but the margins are low.

- It reintroduces the social element of lending.

- A bank may offer a paltry rate of interest for savers while charging borrowers exorbitant rates on personal loans. The bank pockets the difference. Under the P2P model the lender and borrower can agree a rate that is often better for both.

- The facilitator has low costs (no physical branches).

In the current financial climate borrowers are finding it harder to extract loans from the banks. This point alone is likely to turbocharge the expansion of peer to peer lending in future years, but how safe is it in practice?

Sites will vary and it is up to the individual lender to research the experience of other lenders via the comments section and choose wisely. Many offer several reassurances such as:

- Borrower identity checks, credit checks and risk assessments.

- Risk diversification: money spread across a number of borrowers.

- A collections agency.

- An estimate of the bad debt you're likely to experience.

So what is the current bad debt rate? Surprisingly low, if the figures are to be believed. If you take zopa.com as an example, it claims to be running at approximately one to two per cent, having tightened up its criteria over the last few years after a five per cent blip in 2008, but these are average figures and individual returns may vary. One would suggest treading cautiously and letting the reality of the actual returns guide future decisions. The facilitator charges a not insignificant one per cent per annum so this needs to be added in to any calculation. The average overall return is around seven per cent after fees and bad debt.

Zopa is not the only option. There are several other big players including, in the US, prosper.com, which claims to be the world's largest but lenders must be wary:

> 'Prosper says its default rate on loans between November 2005 through Oct. 16, 2008 was 16.5% as of Dec. 31.'

The figure of 16.5 per cent is 'Ouch!', territory. Prosper is now advertising a healthier 10.69 per cent net return (after defaults and service charges) but this new figure is only since 15 July 2009 (which conveniently removes the old high default rates stated above). Remember, unlike the banks, the taxpayer won't bail you out if there is a default.

The point is, if it appeals, try it out and see. What better way to stick two fingers up at the banks than by stealing their business? And what's more, the borrowers will be eternally grateful.

❝ *R£V£NG£ is a dish best served cold.* **❞ Proverb**

Just make sure that you are happy with the prospective net returns after the fees and default rates are removed – bearing in mind no one knows what the default rates will be in the future.

And if you are getting involved in that, why not go all the way and print your own money? Totnes, Brixton, Bristol, and Lewes have. As one uncouth wooden puppet emanating from the 16th century would say, *'That's the way to do it.'*

The Brixton Pound

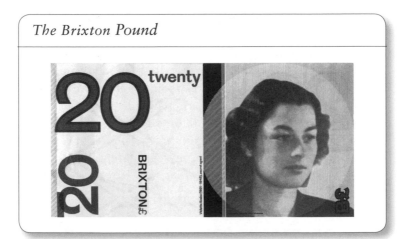

TRIPWIRES ET AL.

Contemplating the future is fine, predicting it is dangerous; as Samuel Goldwyn once said, *'Never make forecasts, especially about the future.'*

Clearly, not knowing the future (or the past) is no excuse for not making a decision, otherwise no one would ever do anything. Certain actions have consequences and so it's time to tread the line between those and the unknown. The unknown unknowns remain exactly that.

The bigger picture either looks gloomy or fantastic, depending on your disposition or what it says on your day release forms. What is clear is that the future is unlikely to be a linear extrapolation of the past. We live in disruptive times and they are becoming more so, not less. As an investor or, more importantly, as a human being, one should at least have one eye on what I will kindly call 'The Tripwires' – major influences that could have considerable impact on the investment world and more importantly the world around you. These are the *'all bets are off'* nominees that no one can afford to ignore.

You may remember that we are predisposed to under-reacting to circumstances that we can't easily recall. Some of these problems appear to be predicaments that have outcomes, not solutions, and there has been little or no preparation by our glorious leaders. In addition, the exponential function is an abstract concept that we struggle to understand and systemic risk is often 'invisible' to the naked eye. So where are the tripwires, what are the bombs and is there any salvation?

First we have the world population. This is a big problem for the planet, and by association each of us, but ironically possibly 'good' in the short to medium term for investors, i.e. the number of consumers is increasing. Providing we don't have a pandemic or natural disaster that wipes out half the population this looks like being the biggest influencer of them all in the longer term. But as usual sensible discussions on the matter seem to be in the taboo category.

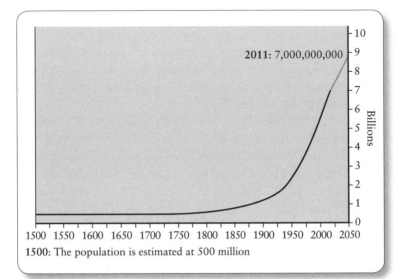

1500: The population is estimated at 500 million

Note: Population data are based on estimates by the UN Population Division and calculations provided by the UN Population Fund.

I can't remember everything about my mathematical studies but do recall having briefly covered population modelling. Every graph I saw that had a population spike had a sharp down slope that matched the up slope. But clearly humankind is rewriting the rules and there is absolutely nothing to worry about – especially the exponential function – as someone has made a prediction that it's going to peak at ten billion. No problem then?

> ❝ *In the same way, democracy cannot survive overpopulation. Human dignity cannot survive overpopulation. Convenience and decency cannot survive overpopulation. As you put more and more people into the world, the value of life disappears.* ❞ **Asimov**

Readers may care to watch Professor Albert Bartlett's incisive video, *Arithmetic, Population and Energy* which debunks much of the guff and piffle spouted on the topic via basic mathematics and observes:

> 'Can you think of any problem in any area of human endeavour on any scale, from microscopic to global, whose long-term solution is in any demonstrable way aided, assisted, or advanced by further increases in population, locally, nationally, or globally?'

Secondly, we have the economy and a debt bomb and, yes, it's our old friend the exponential function.

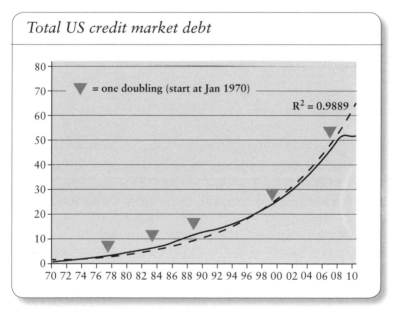

Source: ChrisMartenson.com

Debt has mathematical limits and it looks like we have hit them. You cannot keep increasing the money supply at a disproportionate rate to the increase in actual goods and services without severe consequences. John Greer claims:

> *'There are not enough goods and services on Earth to equal, at current prices, more than a small percentage of the face value of stocks, bonds and derivatives and other fiscal exotica now in circulation.'*

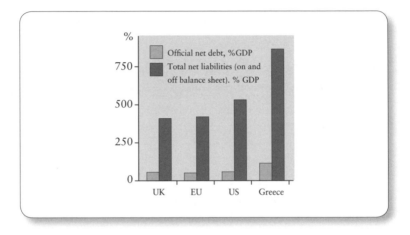

You yourself can borrow money and pay the capital and interest, or you can just pay the interest. When you can't even pay the interest you have a problem. Well, actually you don't, you have a predicament and a Ponzi. But of course, when it comes to stealing from the future, the predicament is far worse because most government statistics have been so manipulated over time as to be meaningless. The official debt figures (see above) are an understated fantasy.

Readers should recall the framing issue from Chapter 3 and remember that **'statistics are like bikinis. What they reveal is suggestive, but what they conceal is vital'** (Aaron Levenstein).

But obviously as an individual you don't need to take any action on these events as we don't recall anything that bad happening with respect to the money supply and, as we saw in Chapter 2, there is no systemic risk whatsoever. For those who don't believe this to be quite the case, have a word with Doug Casey; he thinks geographical diversification of your assets, especially if you live in the West, isn't just a good idea – it's absolutely essential if you want to avoid monetary extinction.

Thirdly we have energy supply and in particular, oil. There is plenty of bad news on the horizon as far as oil is concerned and, guess what? Many people in positions of power are still in denial about it, intentionally or otherwise.

> **"** *The first responsibility of a leader is to define reality.* **"** **Max DePree**

Under this definition we are now leaderless because reality is the last thing that's currently being dished up to the masses in all areas, never mind oil. Leadership is now strictly a grass roots movement. What are you personally going to do about that?

Oil is a finite resource and unlike metals it is not recyclable, so once you have used a barrel of oil, that's it, it's gone. Eventually at some point it is all going to be used. That's physics for you. However, the pain doesn't start when the oil runs out, it starts when demand outstrips supply, i.e. there is not enough to go around. And guess what? We may already be there. It's not the end of oil but it is the end of cheap oil and the start of a headache.

This point was first highlighted in 1956 by a geophysicist called Dr M. King Hubbert. By analysing existing reserves, adding in new discoveries and using production profiles of existing wells, he was able to predict a peak point of production. He predicted that American oil production would peak between 1966 and 1971. The year that America actually reached maximum production was 1970. However, in 1970 most people dismissed Hubbert as a prophet of doom because all they had known was increasing oil production. They were drowning in the stuff, and who doesn't like a good linear extrapolation when it's at home? But this time it's a global issue. **Who could have seen that coming?**

> ❝ *When the mainstream press and government say no-one could have predicted it, they are lying through their f**king teeth.* ❞ **Michael Ruppert,** *Collapse*

There are many excellent books available on the subject and readers are encouraged to familiarise themselves with them, e.g. *Twilight in the Desert* by Matt Simmons. Also look up *The Crash Course* by Chris Martenson and ponder his suggested predicament of *'an economy that must grow meeting an energy system that can't grow.'* The message is essential viewing for everyone on the planet.

This might all sound a little Malthusian* but unlike food black gold is not renewable and we face migrating from a concentrated source of energy to a less concentrated one. If you think this is all a lot of mumbo jumbo, here's a quote from *The Guardian*:

> 'A second senior International Energy Agency [IEA] source, who has now left but was also unwilling to give his name, said there was not as much oil in the world as had been admitted. *'We have [already] entered the "peak oil" zone. I think that the situation is really bad,'* he added.'

Not only have we probably hit the peak (for *conventional* oil; according to the IEA we already passed it in 2006 which is a tad bizarre because in their 2009 report they didn't even mention it), the situation is potentially much worse because in the late 1980s most of the OPEC countries suddenly and miraculously declared massive increases in reserves to try to increase their quotas. According to data from Dr Colin Campbell, in 1988 Iran and Iraq doubled their previously quoted reserves and in

---

* A theory postulated by Thomas Malthus stating that population tends to increase at a faster rate than its means of subsistence and that unless it is checked by moral restraint or disaster (as disease, famine or war) widespread poverty and degradation inevitably result.

1990 Saudi declared 50 per cent more. No external audits have been allowed.

Courtesy of WikiLeaks, one US diplomat confirmed that Saudi Arabia (the largest producer) has overstated their reserves by 40 per cent. This would render more than useless any compensatory arguments that extraction techniques are improving oil yields. Campbell, a former executive with Total of France told a conference: *'If the real [oil reserve] figures were to come out there would be panic on the stock markets ... in the end that would suit no one.'*

Ooops! Tin helmet, anyone? At some point exponential growth will meet finite resources and suddenly the rules of the game will change dramatically. No one knows exactly when this will happen but it is getting harder to argue that it won't (or should that be 'isn't'). And actually impossible if you understand the exponential function – but hey, who cares about simple mathematics?

> 66 *Behind the present rose-tinted facade, the only limitless resources are paper money and propaganda.* 99 **Charles Hugh Smith**

With oil it's about flow rates and how much energy it takes to extract the resource, not just how much there is left. Under 'peak conditions' the oil price is predicted to do pretty much exactly what is happening – a whipsawing in price on an upward trajectory. So here we draw the line between resource depletion and/or overpopulation and technological advancement. What is clear is that the rate of human innovation is likely to increase.

Innovation expands rapidly when communication improves and we have just had the mother of all communication upgrades with the global spread of the internet. Research that 100 years ago would have taken weeks or months to do now takes hours or minutes. A massive expansion in the cross-fertilisation of ideas and generation of new products is occurring. This is the positive news that optimists who think we can engineer our way out of our current problems will look to. It's time to discuss the coming of the second bubble in technology – but this time, it's serious.

Paul Saffo, a Silicon Valley technology forecaster, has postulated a neat theory that every 30 years or so a science migrates into technology we can embrace in our daily lives. So for example Physics, courtesy of Einstein et al., took over from Chemistry as the dominant science in the first half of the 20th century, leading to the atomic bomb, the moon landings, etc. This knowledge allowed for the birth of the transistor chip and electronics took centre stage, culminating in the home computer and the internet. The next science to dominate, Saffo says, will be biology or, put another way, the convergence of nanotech, genetics and robotics into a field that will be *social dynamite*.

What Saffo observes is that inventions take as much as 20 years to migrate from the drawing board to day-to-day usage but, as humans, we are impatient and expect it all to happen much sooner. This delay in adoption (along with, of course, all the other usual bubble suspects) may be a further reason to explain why the 90s' tech bubble got ahead of itself, its profits and just about everything else. The story was right but the timing was out. Remember when **www.** stood for 'world wide wait'?

If you want your future to be challenged by a PowerPoint presentation (surely a contradiction if ever there was one) then watch Juan Enriquez's talk on 'mind boggling new science' for the TED forum at www.ted.com.

In an explosive and very humorous 19 minutes Enriquez argues that the convergence wave of new technology will not only make the financial crisis dissolve into the ultimate re-boot of the economy but the end result will be – a new species of human. Homo Evolutus is defined as *'a hominid that takes direct and deliberate control over the evolution of their species and others.'*

One can argue the timelines and the moralities but biotech, just like the internet, has already had its false dawn and therefore its time is probably coming. Ten years have passed since the detailing of the human genome and now the practical applications are starting to emerge. Individual genome mapping used to cost millions, now it's down to approximately US$50,000 and there is a target to reduce that figure to US$1,000. At that point it's a mass market application.

The possibilities with technological convergence are indeed mind-boggling (and that's without engaging in quantum entanglement). Already people are able to move items on a computer screen by using thought. Add in the fact we can now regrow many body parts and are creating new materials by manipulation at the atomic level (e.g. graphene – who said attempting alchemy was a waste of time?) and it's not going to be too long before hybrid robotics improve on human capabilities. Want an eye that can see in infra-red or ultra violet or at a microscopic level?

The question becomes, 'Will those people who have the means to do so be able to resist physically "upgrading" themselves or their children?' Judging by the insatiable appetite for breast enhancements and genital remodelling it is not hard to guess that certain sections of the global population will welcome it with open legs.

> 66 *It has become appallingly obvious that our technology has exceeded our humanity.* 99 **A. Einstein**

Cue the global Luddites vs technophiles argument. Wealth without health may be worthless, but it seems the former may soon guarantee the latter.

It is highly likely that many solutions will be found to current problems but anyone who thinks the transition from now to the future will be smooth should probably go and stand in the naughty corner with a 'D' for 'Deluded' etched on their conical-shaped millinery. Of course we may all be looking like dunces once the technology singularity is reached. This is the hypothetical point where artificial intelligence exceeds that of humans, an intellectual event horizon. Not sure I want to be around for that one but several proponents think it's coming sometime in the twenty-first century.

RANDOM KINDNESS

After formulating the title *Ouch!* (my proposal had a less acceptable expletive) I thought I had better do a quick search to see what else was out there under this heading and discovered *OUCH: Organisation for the Understanding of Cluster Headaches*. Mmm ... I hope I have made the content engaging and simple enough that the last possible side-effect after reading this book is the manifestation of one of those but for readers who feel that isn't the case, at least you know where the relevant support group is located.

Before signing off there is one experiment we shouldn't forget to mention. Daniel Kahneman, in his book *Thinking, Fast and Slow*, highlights a study where individuals were asked to stand in a room. In the corner was a computer with a screen saver showing money floating in water. Another person then entered the room and dropped some pencils on the floor. The purpose of the experiment? To find out how people's behaviour changed when exposed to money, even if it was just a visual representation. Would the individual be more or less helpful when exposed to the monetary image? The conclusion ... being exposed to money makes us meaner and more independent. We help others less ... essentially, we become more selfish.

Of course the last thing I would want is for anyone reading this book to have become more selfish at the end of it than they were at the beginning. This would be the law of unforeseen consequences in action. I don't know if the reverse is true (watching people being kind encourages others to be the same) but it seems like a reasonable possibility. One antidote to restore the balance is therefore to view Alex Kelly's superb short, *Like*

Other People Do, available online at BBC film network. And then, like its main character, go and indulge in an act of random kindness ...

    ❝ *Be kind, for everyone you meet is*
fighting a hard battle. ❞ **Plato**

I would like to think my own interest in money can be summed up in one word, 'freedom'. The time and money to do what you want, within reason and in a relatively modest way, without having to think about it. But think about it you must. If you want to ignore the signs, abdicate responsibility and continue being an unquestioning slave within the Money Matrix that is your choice, but then be prepared to enjoy the full consequences of doing so.

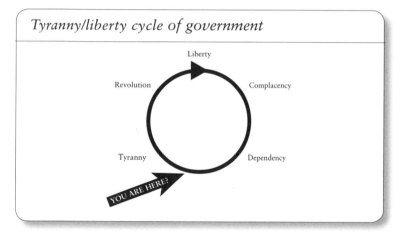

Source: www.examiner.com

Whatever you choose to do with your money or your life I hope this book has at least made an impact in a minor way on your journey (and not just in a 'stick between your spokes' kind of manner). Some of the messages within it may have been a surprise, and not all pleasant ones, but remember, the Mayans got it wrong, it's not the end of the world. There may be some rocky days ahead but as a friend once said, *'If I look forward I'm a pessimist but if I look back I'm an optimist.'* We may simply need to amend our perspectives and if you can't do that, at least be on the right side of the fence. Being pessimistic *and* wrong is a sub-optimal strategy!

For myself, I see a Whitstable sunset, a Jack Russell, and a libation calling. I trust that will be enough to change my perspective, at least for the rest of the day.

Appendix:
Schemes

PONZI

It takes a rare talent to get a scam named after themselves, but Charles Ponzi achieved this particular honour in the 1920s. Bernard Madoff received a 150 year sentence for his 2008 version. *Victims of Ponzi schemes believe that these fraudulent promoters have discovered or developed a 'system' for making money that generates extraordinary returns on investment.* They normally have an element of plausibility that sucks people in.

In the above 'made-off with your money' case it was just a scheme that never actually made any money at all, relying purely on paying out interest from money already donated. *The scheme generates income so long as the pool of investment capital increases faster than the debt accrued.* Ponzi schemes do not decline slowly; they are typically 'massively successful' until they collapse. And collapse they eventually must, it's the law of geometric progression.

BOILER ROOMS

High pressure sales tactics are what gives this scam its name. Often located abroad, a team of 20 to 50 sales people operate out of a single room and are controlled by a 'Stoker' – someone who keeps the pressure on the sales team.

Boilers tend to target those individuals who already own shares. This information is in the public domain and is therefore easy to obtain. Clients (or 'marks') are cold called and while most sensible people will hang up the phone, those that don't will be asked 'what do you do for a living?' Further questions try to establish 'how much they might have to invest'. A classic question is 'Would you be comfortable investing $10,000?' But once into the conversation expect some pressure. One memorable response to a client struggling to find a delaying tactic was as follows:

O   **Client:** '*I would like to discuss this with my wife first*'.

O   **Boiler:** '*Well if you have to go and ask your wife whether you are allowed to buy this, I'm going to have to ring my wife to see if I can sell it to you?*'

Boiler rooms tend to sell 2 types of shares, real ones which are effectively worthless or alternatively shares in a company that doesn't exist. The more professional scams might even send you official looking reports. Either way, the promise of quadrupling your money in 90 days is an empty one. The hoax is continued by informing the victim that the price of the shares has increased and do you want to put more in, or perhaps it later drops but you can get it back by investing more etc. etc. Note to self – Boilers are ugly, keep at arms length.

A dollop of source

CHAPTER 1

BBC news, (2011). 'Millions turn to payday loans, claim insolvency experts.' BBC [online]. Available at: <http://www.bbc.co.uk/news/uk-16063271> [Last updated 7 December 2011.]

Breiter, H. C., *et al.,* (1997). Acute effects of cocaine on human brain activity and emotion. *Neuron*, 19, pp. 591–611.

Breiter, H. C., *et al.,* (2001). Functional imaging of neural responses to expectancy and experience of monetary gains and losses. *Neuron*, 30, pp. 619–639.

Burns, G. S., *et al.,* (2001). Predictability modulates human brain response to reward. *The Journal of Neuroscience*, 21(8), pp. 2793–2798. Available at: <http://www.ccnl.emory.edu/greg/Koolaid_JN_Print.pdf>.

Conway, E., (2009). Reform plan raises fears of bank secrecy. *The Daily Telegraph* [online], 10 January. Available at: <http://www.telegraph.co.uk/finance/newsbysector/banksandfinance/4214232/Reform-plan-raises-fears-of-Bank-secrecy.html>.

Gringon, P., (2006). *Money as debt*. [DVD], available at: <http://www.youtube.com/watch?v=Dc3sKwwAaCU>.

The Guardian, (2009). The Edinburgh home of Sir Fred Goodwin vandalised. *The Guardian* [online], 25 March. Available at: <http://www.guardian.co.uk/business/gallery/2009/mar/25/sir-fred-goodwin-scotland?INTCMP=SRCH>.

Hanke, S. H., (2009). R.I.P. Zimbabwe dollar. The Cato Institute [online]. Available at: <http://www.cato.org/zimbabwe>.

Percival, J. and Carrell, S., (2009). Vandals target Sir Fred Goodwin's house and car. *The Guardian* [online], 25 March. Available at: <http://www.guardian.co.uk/business/2009/mar/25/sir-fred-goodwin-royalbankofscotlandgroup>.

Pytel, G., (2009). The largest heist in history. *Financial crisis? It's a pyramid, stupid* [blog] 13 April. Available at <http://gregpytel.blogspot.com/2009/04/largest-heist-in-history.html>.

Randall, J., (2008). When governments print money, buy gold. *The Daily Telegraph* [online] 18 January. Available at: <http://www.telegraph.co.uk/finance/comment/jeffrandall/2782892/When-governments-print-money-buy-gold.html>.

Rothbard, M. N., (2011). *The case against the fed*. Eastbourne: Terra Libertas.

Rothbard, M. N., (2011). *The mystery of banking*. Eastbourne: Terra Libertas.

Ryan-Collins, J., Greenham, T., Werner, R. and Jackson, A., (2011). *Where does money come from? A guide to the UK monetary system*. London: New Economics Foundation.

The Second Report from the Committee on Laws relating to Lotteries, 1808.

Selgin, G., (2010). *Those dishonest goldsmiths*. University of Georgia. Available at: <http://ssm.com/abstract=1589709>.

Smith, A., (1776). *The wealth of nations*. London: W. Strahan and T. Cadell.

Sundem, G., (2008). How to make better decisions. *BBC News* [online]. Available at: <http://news.bbc.co.uk/1/hi/7238637. stm> [last updated 12:06 on 11 February 2008].

Taruvinga, A., (2011). 'The future of the US dollar', *The Financial Gazette*, 17 August, Zimbabwe.

CHAPTER 2

Batzoglou, F., (2011). Anxious Greeks emptying their bank accounts. *Spiegel Online* [online]. <http://www.spiegel.de/international/europe/0,1518,802051,00.html> [Accessed 12 June 2011].

Berkshire Hathaway Inc., (2002). *Berkshire Hathaway Annual Report, 2002*.

Bootle, R., (1997). *The death of inflation*. London: Nicholas Brealey Publishing.

Cassidy, J., (2010). What good is Wall Street? *The New Yorker* [online]. Available at: <http://www.newyorker.com/reporting/2010/11/29/101129fa_fact_cassidy?currentPage=all> [Accessed 29 November 2010].

Cobb, K., (2011). *The incompetent and the unscrupulous, confidence in the age of MF Global,* [online]. Available at: <http://resourceinsights.blogspot.com/2011/12/incompetent-and-unscrupulous-confidence.html> [Accessed 18 December 2011].

Coggan, P., (2011). *Paper promises, money debt and the new world order.* London: Allen Lane (Penguin).

Cynicuseconomicus, [online]. Available at <http://cynicuseconomicus.blogspot.com/>.

GoldMoneyNews, (2011). Chris *Martenson and James Turk talk about Europe and the global economy.* [video online]. Available at: <http://www.youtube.com/watch?v=BsMj59hyJOQ> [Accessed 3 December 2011].

Grantham, J., (2012). People now see it is a system for the rich only. *Financial Times fm* [online]. Available at: <http://www.ft.com/cms/s/0/c6260c0c-4cb7-11e1-8b08-00144feabdc0.html#axzz1lWtgmm1U> (subscribers only) [Accessed 5 February 2012].

Hayek, F. A., (1944). *The road to serfdom.* New York: George Routledge & Sons.

Huerta de Soto, J., (2006). *Money, bank credit and economic cycles.* Auburn, AL: Ludwig von Mises Institute.

Huitson, O., (2012). The uneconomics guide to money creation. *Silobreaker* [online], 17 February. Available at: <http://www.opendemocracy.net/ourkingdom/oliver-huitson/uneconomics-guide-to-money-creation>.

Mauldin, J. and Tepper, J., (2011). *Endgame The end of the debt supercycle and how it changes everything.* Hoboken, NJ: John Wiley.

The Matrix, (1999). [Film] Directed by Andy Wachowski and Lana Wachowski. USA: Warner Bros.

von Mises, L., (1998). *Human action: A treatise on economics.* Irvington-on-Hudson, NY: Foundation for Economic Education.

MoneyNews, (2011). Jim Rogers: 'Become a farmer. Finance is finished.' *MoneyNews* [online]. Available at: <http://www.moneynews.com/StreetTalk/Rogers-Invest-Natural-Resources/2011/12/08/id/420348> [Accessed 8 December 2011].

Paul, R., (2010). *End the fed*. New York: Grand Central Publishing.

Plender, J., (2009). Shame gene has disappeared from financial system. *Financial Times* [online]. Available at: < http://www.ft.com/cms/s/0/008de884-8a7c-11de-ad08-00144feabdc0.html?nclick_check=1> [Accessed 16 August 2009].

Schlichter, D., (2011). *Paper money collapse*. Hoboken, NJ: John Wiley.

Schlichter, D., (2011). *The nightmare after Christmas*, [online]. Available at: <http://papermoneycollapse.com/2011/12/the-nightmare-after-christmas/> [Accessed 23 December 2011].

Shenker, J., (2011). How youth-led revolts shook elites around the world, *The Guardian* [online], 12 August. Available at: <http://www.guardian.co0.uk/world/2011/aug/12/youth-led-revolts-shook-world>.

Skapinker, M., (2011). 'The Occupy crowd is no match for banks.' *Financial Times*, 9 November.

Stewart, I., (2012). The mathematical equation that caused the banks to crash. *The Guardian* [online], 12 February. Available at: <http://www.guardian.co.uk/science/2012/fcb/12/black-scholes-equation-credit-crunch>.

Taleb, N. N. and Blyth, M., (2011). *The Black Swan of Cairo, Foreign Affairs* [online]. 90(3), May/June.

Turk, J. and Rubino, J., (2004). *The collapse of the dollar and how to profit from it*. New York: Doubleday.

Viz [online]. *Roger's Profanisaurus*. Available at: <http://www.viz.co.uk/profanisaurus.html>.

CHAPTER 3

Ariely, D., (2008). *Predictably irrational.* New York: HarperCollins.

Bartels, A., (2004). Science proves that love is blind. *BBC News* [online]. Available at: <http://news.bbc.co.uk/1/hi/health/3804545.stm> [Last updated 14 June 2004].

Baumeister, R. *et al.*, (2007). The strength model of self control. *Association for Psychological Science*, 16 (6). Available at: <http://bama.ua.edu/~sprentic/101%20Baumeister%20et%20al.%202007-self%20control.pdf>.

Damasio, A. R., (1996). *Descartes' error: emotion, reason, and the human brain.* London: Vintage Books.

Dugatkin, L. A., (2005). *Discovering that rational economic man has a heart* [online]. Available at: <http://www.dana.org/news/cerebrum/detail.aspx?id=748> [Last updated 1 July 2005].

Eisenberger, J. and Liebermann, N. *et al.*, (2006). An experimental study of shared sensitivity to physical pain and social rejection. *PAIN*, 126, pp. 132–138.

Gardner, D., (2009). *Risk.* London: Virgin Books.

Henderson, M., (2009). Probability lessons may teach children how to weigh life's odds and be winners. *The Times* [online]. Available at: <http://www.thetimes.co.uk/tto/education/article1878533.ece> [Accessed 5 January 2009].

Henderson, M., (2009). 'Open-access journal Public Library of Science One.' *The Times*, 24 March.

Horizon, (2009), *How violent are you? Milgrim experiment.* [video online]. Available at: <http://www.youtube.com/watch?v=QhTo3QmB_Yw> and <http://www.youtube.com/watch?v=ISHeON3AsY0&feature=endscreen&NR=1>.

Kahneman, D., (2011). *Thinking, fast and slow*. London: Allen Lane (Penguin).

Montier, J., (2002). *Behavioural finance*. Chichester: John Wiley & Sons.

Montier, J., (2005). Emotion, neuroscience and investing, investors as dopamine addicts. *Global Equity Strategy*, January 20.

Montier, J., (2007). *Behavioural investing*. Chichester: John Wiley & Sons.

O'Connor, R., Power corrupts reason, *TIME Science* [online]. Available at: <http://www.time.com/time/health>.

Piattelli-Palmarini, M., (1994). *Inevitable illusions: How mistakes of reason rule our minds*. New York: John Wiley & Sons.

Schaffhausen, J. *The strange tale of Phineas Gage* [online]. Available at: <http://brainconnection.positscience.com/topics/?main=fa/phineas-gage>.

Shiv, B. and Bechara, A., (2005). Emotions can negatively impact investment decisions. *Stanford Graduate School of Business* [online]. Available at: <http://www.gsb.stanford.edu/news/research/finance_shiv_invesmtdecisions.shtml> [Last updated 1 September 2005].

Slater, L., (2004). *Opening Skinner's box*. London: Bloomsbury.

University of Deakin. Phineas Gage's story. Available at: <http://www.deakin.edu.au/hmnbs/psychology/gagepage/Pgstory.htm>.

Vergano, D., (2006). *USA TODAY* [online]. *Study: emotion rules the brain's decisions*. Available at: <http://www.usatoday.com/tech/science/discoveries/2006-08-06-brain-study_x.htm> [Last updated 8 June 2006].

Wansink, B., Kent, R. J. and Hoch, S. J., (1998). An anchoring and adjustment model of purchase quality decisions. *Journal of Marketing* Research, 35, 71–81, February. Available at: <http://foodpsychology.cornell.edu/pdf/permission/1990-2000/Anchoring-JMR-1998.pdf>.

Westcott, K., (2008). *Raising a glass to pricey wine.* BBC *News* [online]. Available at: <http://news.bbc.co.uk/1/hi/world/americas/7187577.stm> [Accessed 14 January 2008].

Winerman, L. Financial crisis illustrates influence of emotions, behavior on markets. *Online Newshour* [online]. Available at: <http://content.ksg.harvard.edu/lernerlab/media/files/newshour_20081008.pdf>.

CHAPTER 4

Bartels, A., (2004). Science proves that love is blind. *BBC News* [online]. Available at: <http://news.bbc.co.uk/1/hi/health/3804545.stm> [Last updated 14 June 2004].

Barr, A. AIG may have huge gains in second quarter: analyst. *MarketWatch* [online]. Available at: <http://www.marketwatch.com/story/aig-could-have-huge-gains-in-second-quarter-analyst-says/>.

Boffey, D., (2008). Empire in credit crunch. *Daily Mail* [online]. Available at: <http://www.dailymail.co.uk/news/article-1076708/Anthea-Turners-husband-Grant-Bovey-loses-buy-let-empire-credit-crunch.html> [Accessed 11 October 2008].

Cooper, K., (2009). A global depression, or hopes of recovery? *The Times* [online], 15 February. Available at: <http://www.timesonline.co.uk/tol/money/investment/article5732469.ece?token=null&offset=0&page=1>.

Herman, E. S. and Chomsky, N., (1988). *Manufacturing consent.* New York: Pantheon Books.

Levy, C. J., (2011). My family's experiment in extreme schooling. *The New York Times* [online]. Available at: <http://www. nytimes.com/2011/09/18/magazine/my-familys-experiment-in-extreme-schooling.html?_r=1&pagewanted=all> [Accessed 15 September 2011].

Money Box [transcript], BBC, Radio 4, 4 October 2008, 12.00–12.30. Available at: <http://news.bbc.co.uk/1/shared/spl/hi/programmes/money_box/transcripts/08_10_04.pdf>.

Mihm, S., (2008). 'Meet the economist who thinks we're doomed.' *The New York Times*, August 18.

Montier, J., (2005). *Seven sins of fund management.* London: Dresdner Kleinwort Wasserstein.

Montier, J., (2007). *Behavioural investing.* Chichester: John Wiley & Sons.

CHAPTER 5

Anderson, P., (2008). Property will fall until at least 2011. Then US stocks will lead the way. *MoneyWeek* [online]. Available at: <http://www.moneyweek.com/news-and-charts/economics/property-will-fall-until-at-least-2011-then-us-stocks-will-lead-the-way-13814> [Accessed 10 October 2008].

Anderson, P. J., (2008). *The secret life of real estate and banking: how it moves and why.* London: Shepheard-Walwyn.

Bolton, A., (2007). Remember the wisdom of Keynes and Maynard. *Spectator.co.uk* [online]. Available at: <http://www. spectator.co.uk/printer-friendly/31722/remember-the-wisdom-of-keynes-and-mark-twain.thtml> [Accessed 6 June 2007].

Bolton, A., (2009). *Investing against the tide*. Harlow: FT Prentice Hall.

Bonner, B., (2009). *The Daily Reckoning*, 14 April.

C-Span Video Library. *President Franklin D. Roosevelt inaugural address, 4 March 1933*. [video online]. Available at: <http://www.c-spanvideo.org/program/5792-1>.

Fergusson, A., (1975). *When money dies*. London: William Kimber & Co.

Ferguson, J., (2011). 'Ignore inflation – deflation is the real threat to your wealth.' *MoneyWeek*, 565, 25 Nov.

Garrett, G., (2009). *A bubble that broke the world*. Boston, MA: Little, Brown and Co.

Greer, J. M., (2011). *The wealth of nature*. Gabriola Island, BC: New Society Publishers.

Harrison, F., (2007). *Boom bust: house prices, banking and the depression of 2010*. London: Shepheard-Walwyn.

Huettel, S. A., Mack, P. B. and McCarthy, G., (2002). Perceiving patterns in random series: dynamic processing of sequence in prefrontal cortex. Nature Publishing Group [online]. Available at: <http://www.biac.duke.edu/library/papers/2002_NatNeurosci_Huettel.pdf> [Published online 8 April 2002].

Jung, A., (2009). Germany in the era of hyperinflation. *Spiegel Online* [online]. Available at: <http://www.spiegel.de/international/germany/0,1518,641758,00.html> [Accessed 14 August 2009].

Keynes, J. M., (2007). *The economic consequences of peace*. New York: Skyhorse Publishing.

Kimelman, J., (2009). *Jim Rogers isn't buying a U.S. stock recovery.* Barrons.com [online], 20 April.

Kunstler, J. H., (2009). 'State of cringe.' Available at: <http://kunstler.com/blog/2009/01/state-of-cringe.html> [Accessed 26 January 2009].

Mihm, S., (2008). Dr. Doom. *The New York Times* [online]. Available at: <http://www.nytimes.com/2008/08/17/magazine/17pessimist-t.html?_r=1&scp=1&sq=Sept%207th%20 2006%20rubini&st=cse> [Published online 15 August 2008.

Orlov, D., (2011). *Re-inventing collapse.* Gabriola Island, BC: New Society Publishers.

Orlov, D., (2011). The sermon to the sharks. *Energy Bulletin* [online]. Available at: <http://www.energybulletin.net/stories/2011-06-15/sermon-sharks> [Published online 15 June 2011].

Rogoff, K. and Reinhart, C., (2009). *This time is different.* Princeton, NJ: Princeton University Press.

The Schiff Report. *Peter Schiff was right 2006–2007 (2nd edition).* [video online]. Available at: <http://www.youtube.com/watch?v=2I0QN-FYkpw>.

Peter Schiff analogies, (2008). [video online]. Available at: <http://www.youtube.com/watch?v=vweLBpE4mso&feature=related>.

Winerman, L. Financial crisis illustrates influence of emotions, behavior on markets, *Online Newshour* [online]. Available at: <http://content.ksg.harvard.edu/lernerlab/media/files/newshour_20081008.pdf>.

Vekshin, A. and Sterngold, J., (2009). War on Wall Street as congress sees returning to Glass-Steagall. *Bloomberg* [online]. Available at: <http://www.bloomberg.com/apps/news?pid=n

ewsarchive&sid=aeQNTmo2vHpo> [Accessed 27 December 2009].

CHAPTER 6

Arnott, R., (2009). 'Research affiliates.' *FTfm supplement*, August.

Bennett, T., (2008). 'The great stock swindle.' *MoneyWeek*, 411, 21 November.

Bogle Financial Markets Research Center [online]. 'The relentless rules of humble arithmetic.' Available at: <http://www.vanguard.com/bogle_site/sp20060101.htm>.

Castles, C., (2008). Fund managers... like sheep to slaughter. *The Guardian* [online]. Available at: <http://www.guardian.co.uk/money/2008/nov/08/letters-consumer-affairs-john-lewis> [Accessed 8 November 2008].

Dyson, T., (2010). How to profit on America's new era of turbulence. *Daily Wealth* [online]. Available at: <http://www.dailywealth.com/399/How-to-Profit-on-America-s-New-Era-of-Turbulence> [Accessed 10 February 2010].

Frisby, D., (2011). The most dangerous bubble of all. MoneyWeek [online]. Available at: <http://www.moneyweek.com/investments/bonds/government-bond-bubble-13901> [Accessed 21 September 2011].

Godt, N. As goes January, so goes the year? *MarketWatch* [online]. Available at: <http://www.marketwatch.com/news/story/goes-january-so-goes-year/story.aspx?guid=%7BDCD8631C-2889-4F4B-ABD0-07D1EC008F03%7D>.

Heaton, C. S., (2009). 'Buy current yield, not potential growth.' *MoneyWeek*, 428, 27 March.

Kay, J., (2009). *The long and short of it*. London: Erasmus Press.

Keynes, J. M., (2008). *The general theory of employment, interest and money*. www.bnpublishing.com.

Lefèvre, E., (2010). *Reminiscences of a stock operator*. Hoboken, NJ: John Wiley & Sons.

Mauldin, J., (2009). Just desserts and markets being silly again. *The Big Picture* [online]. Available at: <http://www.ritholtz. com/blog/2009/11/just-desserts-and-markets-being-silly-again/>. [Accessed 3 November 2009].

Masonson, L. N., (2011). *All about market timing*. New York: McGraw-Hill Professional.

Mauldin, J., (2009). Thoughts from the frontline newsletter. *Outside the Box*, 3 November.

McQuinsey Quartley, (2009). Surveying the economic horizon.; a conversation with Robert Shiller. *McQuinsey Quarterly* [online]. Available at: <http://www.mckinseyquarterly.com/Economic_Studies/ Productivity_Performance/Surveying_the_economic_horizon_A_ conversation_with_Robert_Shiller_2345>.

Powley, T., (2009). Scrap TERs for up-front calculation, demands Miller. *FT Advisor* [online]. Available at: <http://www. ftadviser.com/2011/10/26/investments/uk/scrap-ters-for-up- front-calculation-demands-miller-oCJO3RnPyTjGKvdCr4nfkI/ article.html> [Accessed 19 October 2009].

Price, T., (2009). *Why long-term stock market returns are an illusion*. The Price Report (subscriber only newsletter), 57, 9 July.

Price, T., (2009). What baseball and the stock market have in common. Seeking Alpha [online]. Available at: < http://seekingalpha. com/article/156097-what-baseball-and-the-stock-market-have-in- common> [Accessed 14 August 2009].

Price, T., (2009). *The 5 biggest questions in finance.* The Price Report (subscriber only newsletter), 61, 3 September.

Rogoff, K. and Reinhart, C., (2008). 'The aftermath of financial crises.' University of Maryland and Harvard University.

Shiller, R., Robert Shiller online data. Available at: <http://www. econ.yale.edu/~shiller/data/ie_data.xls>.

Somerset Webb, M., (2008). *Love is not enough: a smart woman's guide to money.* London: Harper Perennial.

Stock Market Crash, (2008). 'What causes a stock market crash? And what can you do?' Stock Market Crash [online]. Available at: <http://stockmarketcrash.net/> [Accessed 12 August 2008].

The Quotable Sir John Templeton – on life and spirituality. Available at: <http://www.sirjohntempleton.org/quotes.asp>.

Undercover Economist, (2008). More on market timing. *FT.com* [online]. Available at: <http://blogs.ft.com/undercover/2008/ 10/more-on-market-timing/#axzz1eT5ggCHc>. [Accessed 15 October 2008].

Volatility S&P 500. Available at: <http://finance.yahoo.com/ echarts?s=%5EVIX#chart2:symbol=^vix;range=my;indicator =volume;charttype=line;crosshair=on;ohlcvalues=0;logscale= on;source=undefined>.

CHAPTER 7

Bonner, B., (2007). *Mobs, messiahs and markets.* London: John Wiley & Sons.

Bradt, S., Brain takes itself on over immediate vs. delayed gratification. *Harvard University Gazette* [online]. Available at: <http://www.news.harvard.edu/gazette/2004/10.21/07-brain battle.html>.

The Terry Wallis Fund [online]. Available at: <http://www.the
terrywallisfund.org/history.html>.

Huettel, S. A., Mack, P. B. and McCarthy, G., (2002). Perceiving
patterns in random series: dynamic processing of sequence in
prefrontal cortex. Nature Publishing Group [online]. Available at:
<http://www.biac.duke.edu/library/papers/2002_NatNeurosci_
Huettel.pdf> [Publishing online 8 April 2002].

Hugh Smith, C., (2011). *An unconventional guide to investing in
troubled times*. CreateSpace.

McClure, S. M., Laibson, D. I. *et al.,* (2004). Separate neural
systems value immediate and delayed monetary rewards.
Science, 306, 15 October. Available at: <http://www.csbmb.
princeton.edu/ncc/PDFs/Neural%20Economics/McClure%20
et%20al%20(Science%2004).pdf>.

Montier, J., (2007). *Behavioural investing.* Chichester: John
Wiley & Sons.

msnbc.com. *Man's brain rewired itself in 19 years after crash.*
msnbc.com [online]. Available at <http://www.msnbc.msn.com/
id/13690450/>.

Wark, P., (8 April 2004). How I confounded the autism experts: I
rewired my son's brain. *The Times* [online]. Available at: <http://
www.thetimes.co.uk/tto/life/article1716149.ece>.

Zweig, J., (2007). *Your money and your brain.* New York: Simon
and Schuster.

CHAPTER 8

Albert, A. Bartlett [online]. Available at: <http://www.albartlett.
org/index.html>.

Church, N., (2006). Thinking the unthinkable. *Countercurrents. org* [online]. Available at: <http://www.countercurrents.org/po-church170706.htm> [Accessed 17 July 2006].

Discover Magazine. The end of divorce? Growing numbers of people marrying inanimate objects. *Discover Magazine* [online]. Available at: <http://blogs.discovermagazine.com/discoblog/2009/04/13/the-end-of-divorce-growing-numbers-of-people-marrying-inanimate-objects/>.

GoldMoney. Chris Martenson's presentation at the Gold & Silver meeting in Madrid. [video online]. Available at: <http://www.goldmoney.com/video/martenson-presentation.html>.

Hugh Smith, C., (2011). *An unconventional guide to investing in troubled times.* CreateSpace.

Hunt, B., (2009). You'll lose every single time if you buy these ETFs. *The Daily Wealth*, 20 December. Available at: <http://www.dailywealth.com/8/You-ll-Lose-Every-Single-Time-if-You-Buy-These-ETFs>.

Jackson, T., (2011). Good old days when bonuses were paid from profits. *Financial Times* [online]. Available at: <http://www.ft.com/cms/s/0/83ce603a-017a-11e1-b177-00144feabdc0.html#axzz1tjEkImFm> (subscriber only)[Accessed 31 October 2011].

John Williams' Shadow Government Statistics [online]. Available at: <http://www.shadowstats.com/>.

Jung, A., (2009). Germany in the era of hyperinflation. *Spiegel Online* [online]. Available at: <http://www.spiegel.de/international/germany/0,1518,641758,00.html>. [Accessed 14 August 2009].

Kahneman, D., (2011). *Thinking, fast and slow.* London: Allen Lane.

Kelly, A., (2008). Like other people do. [video online]. BBC [online]. Available at: <http://www.bbc.co.uk/filmnetwork/films/p006hqsp>.

Eric Kraus [online]. Available at: <http://nikitskyfund.com/files/tnb/TB_Meetings%20with%20Remarkable%20Men_Sep2009_eng.pdf>.

Lefèvre, E., (2010). *Reminiscences of a stock operator.* Hoboken, NJ: John Wiley & Sons.

Macalister, T., (2009). Key oil figures were distorted by US pressure, says whistleblower. *The Guardian* [online]. Available at: <http://www.guardian.co.uk/environment/2009/nov/09/peak-oil-international-energy-agency/print>. [Accessed 9 November 2009].

Maloney, M., (2008). *Guide to investing in gold and silver.* New York: Grand Central Publishing.

Mauldin, J. and Tepper, J., (2011). *Endgame: the end of the debt supercycle and how it changes everything.* Hoboken, NJ: John Wiley & Sons.

MoneyNews, (2011). Jim Rogers: 'Become a farmer. Finance is finished.' MoneyNews [online]. Available at: <http://www.moneynews.com/StreetTalk/Rogers-Invest-Natural-Resources/2011/12/08/id/420348>. [Accessed 8 December 2011].

Seeking Alpha. *Contrarian Profits.* Seeking Alpha [online]. Available at: <http://seekingalpha.com/author/contrarian-profits>.

TED. Juan Enriquez shares mindboggling science, 2009. [video online]. Available at: <http://www.ted.com/talks/juan_enriquez_shares_mindboggling_new_science.html>.

The New Wave Slave, (2011). *Marc Farber on the Fed & Gold.* [video online]. Available at: <http://www.youtube.com/watch?v=LMxJ8_9Htfw>.

Vidal, J., (2011). WikiLeaks cables: Saudi Arabia cannot pump enough oil to keep a lid on prices. *The Guardian* [online]. Available at: <http://www.guardian.co.uk/business/2011/feb/08/saudi-oil-reserves-overstated-wikileaks/ > [Accessed 8 February 2011].

Index